FRAGMENTS *of* PARADISE

ALSO BY PAUL AND AUDREY GRESCOE

Alaska: The Cruise-Lover's Guide (1994)

BY PAUL GRESCOE

The Money Rustlers: Self-made Millionaires of the New West (1985, with David Cruise)
Jimmy: An Autobiography (1987, with Jimmy Pattison)
Flesh Wound (1991)
Songs from the Wild (1992, with Karl Spreitz)
Blood Vessel (1993)
Vancouver: Visions of a City (1993, with Karl Spreitz)

FRAGMENTS *of* PARADISE

BRITISH COLUMBIA'S WILD AND
WONDROUS ISLANDS

Paul and Audrey Grescoe

RAINCOAST BOOKS

Vancouver

BEAUTIFUL
BRITISH COLUMBIA
Magazine

First published in 1995 by

Raincoast Book Distribution Ltd.
8680 Cambie Street
Vancouver, B.C.
V6P 6M9

Beautiful British Columbia
929 Ellery Street
Victoria, B.C.
V9A 7B4

CANADIAN CATALOGUING IN PUBLICATION DATA

Grescoe, Paul, 1939-
Fragments of paradise

ISBN 1-55192-002-6 (bound) – ISBN 1-55192-000-x (pbk.)

1. Pacific Coast (B.C.) – Description and travel. 2. Islands –
British Columbia. I. Grescoe, Audrey. II. Title.
FC3845.P2G73 1995   917.11'1   C95-910403-8
F1089.P2G73 1995

Designed by Dean Allen
Project Editor: Michael Carroll
Copy Editor: Jacqueline Wood
Maps by Eric Leinberger

*This book is printed on acid-free paper produced from selectively harvested trees. No
clearcut, rainforest, or other endangered-species products were used. The
manufacturing process involves no dioxin-producing chlorine.*

Printed and bound in Hong Kong

For Kay Patterson

USA
CANADA

Dixon Entrance

Masset

QUEEN

Skidegate

CHARLOTTE

Hecate Strait

ISLANDS

QUEEN
CHARLOTTE
ISLANDS
Page 86

B R I T I S H

*Princess
Royal
Island*

C O L U M B I A

Queen

Charlotte

Bella Bella

Bella Coola

Sound

Rivers Inlet

INSIDE
PASSAGE
ISLANDS
Page 56

Queen Charlotte Strait

Cape
Scott

Port Hardy

VANCOUVER ISLAND

P A C I F I C

Campbell
River

Powell
River

Squamish

O C E A N

*Clayoquot
Sound*

*Gambier
Island*

Port Alberni

Strait of Georgia

Bowen Island

Vancouver

Nanaimo

GULF
ISLANDS Page 24

Duncan

CANADA
USA

Cowichan Bay

Neah Bay

Sooke

Victoria

WASHINGTON

Strait of Juan de Fuca

Port
Angeles

Port Townsend

N

W   E

S

0   50 miles

0   50 kilometres

CONTENTS

CHRIS CHEADLE

ACKNOWLEDGEMENTS

W E WOULD LIKE to thank our son, Taras Grescoe, for researching and writing – with his usual skill and stylishness – the section on Malcolm Island; Chuck and Sheila Herman, dear
friends who have given us so many splendid days on Savary Island; Paul and
Loretta Minvielle, old buddies who were willing to open up their lives to us;
new friends Laurence and Jan Gough, for the loan of their cottage on the
sea to write some of this book; chum Alan Edmonds, for his background on
the Sideras colony; Sid Marty, writer and ex-park warden, for permission to
quote from his wonderful journal about Kermode bears; Des Kennedy, for
permission to quote from his *Living Things We Love to Hate*; Jeff King of the
Queen Charlotte Islands Observer, for his insights; David Phillips of the
Copper Beach House in Masset, for his hospitality; Doug, Ian, and Rosie
Gould of Moresby Explorers, for their transportation and hospitality in the
Charlottes; Bob Hagman, who told us so much about Texada Island; helpful
realtors Juanita Chase of Savary, Paddy and Bob Gee of Hornby, John Yuill
of Colliers Macaulay Nicolls, and Doug Clarke of Henley and Associates,
who flew Audrey to Dayman Island and shared his knowledge of privately
owned islands; Bill Embrey of Harbour Air, who flew an ailing Paul out of
Gwaii Haanas; islanders Brad and Julie Ovenell-Carter, Ross Allan, Bob
Andrew, Nick Bantock, Doug Berry, Patrick Brown, Marilyn and Jonathan
Chilvers, Wolfgang Duntz, Edythe Hanen, Douglas Hooper, Ross Johnson,
Jeanette Murdoch, Susan Nicholson, Briony Penn, Lynn and Brock Piper,
Don Reeves, Alan Robertson, Martin Rogers, Mike Stacey, and Barry
Valentine; mainlanders Conn Andrie, Peter Leech, provincial toponymist
Janet Mason, futurist Frank Ogden, and Mary Powell; generous-spirited
John Thomson of *Beautiful British Columbia* and irrepressible photograph-
er/designer Karl Spreitz, who were so intimately and vitally involved in the
beginnings of this book; and finally Mark Stanton, Michael Carroll, and
Dean Allen of Raincoast Books, who made it happen so well.

*Fairfax Point on Moresby Island,
one of the southernmost Gulf
Islands, looking east to
Washington State's
Mount Baker.*

RUSS HEINL

THE LAST SWEET ESCAPE

I T I S J U N E 20, a day before the start of our 54th summer, and we're lolling in a tea-and-toast stupor on the deck of a shake-sheathed cabin on an island in the Strait of Georgia. The sun is bestowing its early-morning benediction, and the breeze is as soft as the white wisp of gull's feather lilting just out of our reach. A couple of strides away (as if we had the will to move), a flashy rufous hummingbird is cruising the purple fox-glove thrusting from the sand; on the croissant of shore beyond, a pair of patrolling eagles swaps places on boulders revealed overnight by the retreating tide. Out there, a quartet of seals mirrors our indolence, basking in place, flippers rearing from time to time as they rearrange themselves on the rocks. The wide-screen view, framed by young spruce and cedar, is of the pitted liquid steel of the Pacific, and layers of the Coast Mountains sil-houetted in watercolour shades of wash-blue. For one bad moment, their serrated peaks remind us of the jagged lines of the electrocardiogram charts that we have seen too many of in recent weeks. But that image vanishes as fast as the hummingbird has. What remain are the sun and the scents and the satin air – balm for both soul *and* heart. We are content to sit here, all but motionless, swathed in the setting, for the next 10 days, if not eternity. "You know," Audrey says, "there've been a lot of holidays in our life, but there hasn't been enough beach time."

Beaches like this one help define, literally and figuratively, the thou-sands of islands and islets that punctuate the north Pacific off the British Columbia mainland from the Strait of Georgia to the Gulf of Alaska. To many of us who have moved to this corner of the country (and even those born here), the islands represent an ultimate escape hatch: one last sweet place where we can be when the world overwhelms us. Individually and col-lectively, they meet Vancouver humorist Eric Nicol's definition of an island as "a piece of land completely surrounded by envy." For here there are

Private islands, like this one amid the Gulfs, is – in the words of one inhabitant – "like having your own country."

islands with the settings and microclimates, the sad and salty histories, and the rare contemporary lifestyles to meet most urban dreamers' visions: beaches of wave-smoothed pebbles and sand, strewn with silvered logs from the evergreened mountains that form the inevitable backdrop; salmon-plucking eagles and sunbathing seals, with the promise of killer whales cavorting off the front yards of waterfront homes, and the only natural threat the deer poaching in the back gardens. Beach time means blissed-out days of determinedly doing nothing in the sun, except digging for clams and plumbing tide pools. And at night there are communal bonfires where the sounds of guitar or harmonica backstop the old songs, while cold beer and hot coffee are sipped, burnt marshmallows and butter-sodden popcorn passed around, and the phosphorescence illuminating the water competes with the sparks of crackling driftwood.

There can be a timelessness here, a sense of apartness on Canada's westernmost islands. Cocooned from the continent, they are linked only by the sometime floatplanes and the ubiquitous boats and the intricate system of ferries, which are made to be missed – as though missing them were a kind of nose-thumbing at the structure imposed by their schedules. (Islands, a friend says, are all about having an excuse to miss connections. When Hornby Island artist Wayne Ngan went beachcombing after arriving too late for a ferry, he found a remnant of a moon-snail shell, whose shape later inspired him to do a small bronze sculpture.)

This separation, as psychological as it is physical, has created singular ways of life pursued by the singular people who have chosen to live on such singular isles.

The islands celebrated here, in our words and in pictures by some of British Columbia's finest photographers, range in character and geography from the people-pressured southern Gulf Islands to the underpopulated, isolated Queen Charlottes just below Alaska, and in between them the myriad diverse islands of the Inside Passage. We have purposefully ignored Vancouver Island, "the Island," which, with a population of nearly 600,000 in 32,000 square kilometres, is more than five times the size of the province of Prince Edward Island.

Although we called this book *Fragments of Paradise: British Columbia's Wild and Wondrous Islands*, we could have used any number of adjectives in the title, including "lovely" and "livable," "beautiful" and "blessed." They do rank among – if not at the pinnacle of – the world's most blessed. As far back as 1953, in his book *One Million Islands for Sale*, American Robert Froman singled them out as special: ". . . the British Columbia islands offer the best and the most chances to escape to an island on the continent's west coast." The distinction still stands. Here nature is almost

Sea lions on Reef Island, near the abandoned Native village of Skedans, Queen Charlotte Islands.

2

GRAHAM OSBORNE

3

embarrassingly munificent, food (as First Nations fishermen found) can be plentiful, and any contemporary poverty is usually self-imposed. The islands lure innumerable weekenders and vacationers who use their sports (boating, hiking, hunting, fishing) as convenient excuses to surround themselves for a bittersweet time in beauty. It is the same embracing, self-contained beauty that seduces an inordinate share of artists of every discipline to live here year-round: painters, potters, weavers, musicians, writers, photographers.

Graham Osborne and Russ Heinl are among those many photographers who have a love affair with these islands – even though one of them lives on the mainland and the other on Vancouver Island. Their work is represented in this book. The lengths to which they went to record their riveting images of the islands can be summed up in two stories. Graham was photographing in the Queen Charlottes, just north of the abandoned Haida island of Skungwai, from a twin-outboard boat operated by wardens of the Gwaii Haanas National Park Reserve and Haida Heritage Site. They dropped him off on a shoreline "like a big rock garden" to capture a fabulous display of red columbine. Although exposed to the full might of the open Pacific, the coast at first was calm. But the wind began rising and after three hours, big whitecaps crashed on the rocks. By the time he returned to the boat, the swells were tall enough to swallow their craft in the troughs. On the tense 15-minute journey back to the inner coast, none of the four seasoned sea travellers spoke a word. As Graham says, with understatement, "the Charlottes can be rugged, beautiful, tempting – and deceptive."

Russ is an experienced aerial photographer who flies with the Snowbirds, the Canadian Forces stunt team, and has spent hundreds of hours over the islands in a small single-engined Hughes 300 helicopter piloted by Andrew North of Go Island Hopper Helicopters in Victoria. But both men had a feeling of dread the day they went to photograph remote Triangle Island, far off the northwestern coast of Vancouver Island (see page 15). When Russ told Andrew about unaccountably feeling clammy and nauseated, the pilot admitted his unease: "Russ, I can't carry on." The photographer urged him on and reaching the island, they dropped to an altitude of about 75 metres between two points of land. The wind, which had been calm, suddenly picked up speed and grabbed the helicopter – propelling it toward the ocean. Andrew powered downward, going with the wind to gain speed. In the last moments, the chopper pulled out of the dive. "That was very close," Russ said finally. "Any more and we would have been finished," the pilot replied.

Islands in Howe Sound: lovely, livable, beautiful, and blessed.

BOB HERGER

GUNTER MARX

6

THIS IS NEITHER travel guide nor history book, although it offers a smattering of both genres. If anything, it is a personal chronicle, a selective celebration, of how people are living on these islands now. We agree with Mark Salzman, who summed up why he wrote *Iron and Silk*, his Pulitzer Prize-winning book about his two years in China: "To me, a sense of place is nothing more than a sense of people. Whether a landscape is bleak or beautiful, it doesn't mean anything to me until a person walks into it, and then what interests me is how the person behaves in that place."

It takes imagination to make an island into a world and imagination to stay in that world. Failed islanders are diminished by an island's isolation. The departure of the last ferry of the day may have seemed like the slamming of a prison door to them. Successful islanders are ingenious, creative deployers of their own time. For them, reduced resources and lack of stimulation are prods to their inventiveness. They conceive schemes and realize them. Even though the insularity of islands is almost an illusion today, the illusion is enough for those who are able to look inward for inspiration. Roads allow you to drive away to see what they've done in the next town; a surrounding sea sends you back and gives you back to yourself.

"There are always two kinds of people – those who own and are owned by the earth that they touch, and those who float," says Janey Bennett, an architectural historian and landscape designer from Carmel, California. A floater, she has been coming to Hornby Island in the Inside Passage since 1979 and intends to move there soon. "And those who float can imagine themselves living anywhere and can probably pull it off. Those are the people who can go to a new experience such as an island." Such people as David Phillips of Masset in the Queen Charlottes, a big, round greybeard who holds court in his bed-and-breakfast and promotes such extraordinary concepts as replacing the downsized military base in "human-scale" Masset with an agency of the United Nations dealing with the Pacific Rim. "We're a perfect Geneva for the 20th century," he says with not a hint of humour. Way down south off the Sunshine Coast, Dr. Wally Thomas, a retired Vancouver hematologist, owns three-hectare-square Charles Island where he propagates, in a solar-powered, hydroponic greenhouse, one of the continent's three major collections of orchids of the genus called *odontoglossum*. Here in perlite instead of soil he breeds new hybrids (many of which have earned him international awards) and hikes the trails and meadows of his own private fiefdom.

Some, but not all, retirees can imagine living on an island and pull it off; some can't. J. Ray Popkin-Clurman did; his wife didn't. He is a millionaire American television engineer whose company developed automatic balance control for colour television and, in Quebec during the 1940s,

Saturday farmers' market on the Ganges harbourfront, Saltspring Island.

launched what was Canada's first modern TV station. About to retire and wanting to leave overcrowded Long Island, New York, he and his wife moved to Saltspring Island in the late 1970s after they had visited every region chronicled in a newspaper's roster of the seven best places to live in the United States. The list included Washington's San Juans, but even then a waterfront lot in those islands was going for $50,000. Just north of the border, amid the Gulfs, Saltspring was not only much cheaper, he thought it prettier. With a local partner, he and three Long Island friends bought 800 metres of Beaver Point shoreline, 1.6 kilometres deep, for $750,000 and developed it into 70 one-fifth-hectare parcels. One friend, a dental surgeon, moved his practice to the island. At the time, there were perhaps 1,200 people on Saltspring, and Ray quickly blended into island society, befriending, among others, Barbara Wedgewood, heiress to the British pottery-family fortune, who drove around in a Rolls-Royce and built an English country home that later became the plush Ganges resort, Hastings House. After Ray's wife left him and the island – "for her, it was an intellectual wilderness" – fellow ham-radio buffs threw a couple of cocktail parties where he met more than 100 women. "For a while I was very busy," he told us. "I acquired a yellow New York taxicab, so the gossips on the island were very effective in keeping track of my movements." He has since married twice more and, although many other islanders have complained about the overcrowding and moved on, Ray – perhaps recalling the other island he once lived on – says, "We're very satisfied here."

And then there's us. Like the others, we are islomanes, a word promulgated by Lawrence Durrell, the British novelist who so loved the Greek Isles. It means "people who are crazy about islands" and it is, as Vancouver Island poet Charles Lillard says, one of the loveliest words in the English language. Islomanes for more than a quarter century, we have retreated often to the islands off our West Coast. Mayne Island was the first – a waterfront cottage holiday 25 years ago with a brace of parents and our two-year-old son. We ate our first raw oysters there and discovered the fun of combing the beach for treasures the tide had deposited; once it brought us a new saucepan, which we adopted and used for many years. When the children were young, we camped at Galiano Island's Montague Harbour and rented a doctor's house on Saltspring. When they were grown, we chose Tree Tops, a romantic bed-and-breakfast on Galiano, and Hastings House, the Relais & Châteaux inn on Saltspring, to help us celebrate advanced wedding anniversaries. Savary Island was where we cycled on sandy roads with old friends and sat on a beach calling to the Northern Lights. Pender was a novel written during long, quiet days in a house on the sea. And Bowen, in our 54th autumn, was to become our new home.

FOR SALE: PRIVATE
ISLAND WITH A PAST

JUST WEST OF GALIANO in the Gulf Islands, the 49th parallel passes through Reid and Thetis islands and north of perfect little Dayman Island. In 1852 a Portuguese immigrant named Joe Silvey bought Reid's 97 hectares for $2.60. In 1994, 9.7-hectare Dayman was on the market – for $2,600,000.

Private islands like Dayman (population: three) inevitably spawn stories, about resident hermits and duchesses, about mystics and gamblers, about royalty and hidden gold. Dayman's most interesting story concerns the man who brought LSD to British Columbia: Alfred M. Hubbard. Born in Kentucky in 1902,

Hubbard undertook a series of clandestine ventures along the Pacific Northwest coast, including covert operations for the Office of Strategic Services, the American spy agency. He became a Canadian citizen during the Second World War, eventually moving to Vancouver where in 1955 he was president of Uranium Corporation. The same year, Hubbard bought d-lysergic acid diethylamide from Sandoz Laboratories in Switzerland and, while it was still legal, turned thousands of people on, including clients of Hollywood Hospital, a psychotherapy treatment centre in New Westminster, British Columbia. This secretive but outgoing man owned

Dayman, and visited it frequently with his wife, and perhaps with his friend Timothy "Turn On, Tune In, Drop Out" Leary. When Hubbard sold the island to a syndicate, he left a house – and a hidden trace of his presence.

In the 1970s, a B.C. businessman, Conn Andrie, bought Dayman. He and his wife, Gay, lived there for 10 years with their daughter, Cindy, and son, Stuart (who, but for a 5:00 a.m. floatplane trip to a mainland hospital, would have been born on the island). Having never missed a day boating the children to elementary school on Thetis, even in the dark and fog of winter, the Andries gave up their insular life so the children could attend mainland high schools.

"We had the best years of our lives there," says Andrie. "But it was not easy living on the island. The work never stopped." There were trails to be cut – one

AUDREY GRESCOE

around the perimeter measures exactly 1.6 kilometres – and water to be pumped from a slow-producing well into a storage tank. In an attempt to supply electricity, Andrie installed a custom-built windmill, placing it where favourable winds had been recorded. "The wind never blew for a month and a half," he says. He then brought in hydro and telephone service by underwater cable.

Hubbard had a house on the southeast point facing Thetis and Hudson islands. Andrie replaced it with a handsome three-bedroom, two-bathroom red-cedar design, fronted by a hexagonal tower where he and Gay planned to sit and admire their view when they had time. It was while moving a woodshed that Andrie found Hubbard's souvenir: a gallon jar of LSD capsules – "the pure stuff, labelled Switzerland LSD" – which he turned over to the RCMP.

Like island dwellers everywhere, the Andries exercised their seigneurial rights, christening the points and beaches of their domain. "Every knoll was named," says Andrie. And in an exuberant gesture, they planted a thousand daffodil bulbs in a meadow at North Point, spelling out the children's names so they could be seen from the air.

From our seaplane on a sunny spring morning after daffodil season, Dayman looks like an island in the Caribbean. It wears a necklace of clear jade, water so limpid we can see the underlying rock that supports it like a piece of sculpture on a pedestal. As we circle overhead, the island momentarily takes the shape of a swimming tortoise, its shell an oval of fir and arbutus, its head a point of exposed foreshore stretching south, its feet kicking out to the north.

We land and tie up at a floating dock. The present owner is enjoying a late breakfast with her three black Labradors. In five years on Dayman, she's learned to love island time: "You say you're going to fix the boat but that might be six months from now." At her invitation, we explore, walking around the shoreline in just over an hour, with a pause to admire the seven beaches, each one more seductive than the last.

At North Point, we meet the house-coated caretaker, who is also getting a late start on the day. He mentions some of the island's attractions: in front of his mobile home, an oyster bed (which Conn Andrie still leases); an arbutus tree that four people *might* be able to encircle at the base, its main trunk rising 18.27 metres before it divides – the second-largest arbutus in British Columbia, he's been told; and an astonishing metre-deep soil cover extending 350 metres from the main house to his place.

He leaves us with this thought: "Living on a private island is like having your own country; nothing happens unless you make it happen."

CHRIS CHEADLE

The shedding, rust-hued bark of the arbutus.

R. STEPHENS

We have travelled the coast by sailboat, rowboat, catamaran, kayak, Polaris, Zodiac, and inboard water taxi, by floatplane, helicopter, and Fokker F-28 jet. But mostly we have used the fleet of the BC Ferry Corporation, which as Canada's biggest passenger shipping company operates the province's marine highway. Each year it carries more than 22 million passengers and eight million vehicles. The provincial government launched the service in 1960 after privately owned Canadian Pacific Steamships and the Black Ball Line were locked in labour disputes that threatened to sever their ferry ships' umbilical cord to Vancouver Island. BC Ferries' 40 vessels run in size from the 12.8-metre length and 20.57-gross-ton weight of the *Dogwood Princess II*, linking Gambier and Keats islands to the Sunshine Coast, to the 167.5-metre length and 18,790 gross tons of the super-ferries *Spirit of British Columbia* and *Spirit of Vancouver Island*, which voyage between Tsawwassen on the mainland and Swartz Bay on Vancouver Island. We have come to admire the skilled ferry workers, two-way radios on their belts, who juggle passengers and vehicles in their blue peaked caps and fluorescent vests, and

The Texada Island ferry, one of the smaller of BC Ferries' 40 vessels.

11

T.W.'S IMAGE NETWORK · TIM MATHESON

12

sometimes in sunglasses and Bermuda shorts. There are many beards among them, reflecting the appropriate nautical image and/or the relaxed lifestyles of the islands, where so many of the workers live.

The ferries are more than a seagoing extension of the highways. From the first, they have been an alternate means of communication and sometimes a literal lifeline for islanders. The smaller vessels, in particular, act as mobile bulletin boards. A typical collection of notices, pinned up on the Texada ferry, included advertisements for two desktop-publishing firms on the island; a Christian retreat centre; bookkeeping, gift-basket, and Sheltie-stud services; and announcements of a farmers' market, a mountain-bike race, the Elks Open Fishing Derby, and the annual Sandcastle Weekend. The additional roles the crew of a ferry sometimes take on are nicely illustrated in a story we heard from the husband of a woman who lived on Dayman (see page 9), a minuscule private island amid the Gulfs. Returning in a motorboat after dropping her children off at school on Thetis Island, she got disoriented and panicky in dense fog. The captain of a Gulf Islands ferry spotted her on the radar going in the wrong direction and said, "There goes Gay." After the crew pointed her the right way, she again headed away from Dayman. "There she goes again," the captain remarked, turning back, this time directing her safely home.

The first large craft to work these waters – aside from the immense cedar dugouts in which the Haida travelled – were the European ships that began arriving in the late 18th century. Spain's survey expeditions and Britain's naval sorties (most prominently under Captain George Vancouver) mapped and christened much of this Pacific coast. Many of the Gulf Islands exemplify that legacy: Galiano and Valdez are named for Spanish naval commanders who explored the area, Saturna for a Spanish schooner, the *Saturnina*; Mayne bears the name of a British surveyor, Thetis and Kuper are the names of a 36-gun British ship and her captain. And Pender is named after a captain who completed the Royal Navy's survey of the coast in 1870.

Captain Daniel Pender worked from the first steamship to run the Inside Passage continuously, the SS *Beaver*, launched in England by the Hudson's Bay Company in 1835. The elm-keeled paddle wheeler, 30 metres long, had several lives: for 26 years, trading for the fur company, with a cannon and large crew to keep the peace; for another eight, surveying the coastline for the Navy; and for her final 20 years in private service, towing lumber and coal ships, supplying lumber camps, and toting passengers. The first cruise ships to carry sight-seeing passengers as well as cargo for the villages and canneries up the coast were lavishly fitted Pacific Coast Steamship vessels. In 1898, the passage was awash in boats of every kind en route to the Yukon gold fields. By then, entrepreneurs had arrived in search of fish and

Floatplanes, like this one off Saltspring, are one of the islands' vital umbilical cords.

lumber, and with them came the workers who stayed to live on British Columbia's islands.

Among the shipping lines that grew to serve them – delivering sides of beef and live poultry and pigs, bales of hay and sacks of mail – were Canadian Pacific, the Grand Trunk Pacific, the All Red Line, British Columbia Steamships, and the Union Steamship Company. Union's logging camp run, launched in 1892, made 40 landings in four days, including Texada, Cortes, Read, Quadra, and East Thurlow islands. One of the early steamers, the 144-passenger *Cassiar*, had an electrically lit loggers' saloon with a smoking room, bar, and lounge. The ships became the islanders' connection to the world in many ways, with their special hospital cabins, travelling newsstands, and bootlegging crew members. By the 1930s, despite the Depression, Union Steamships was also solidly in the excursion business, making day trips to Bowen Island, the Sunshine Coast, and Savary Island ("the South Sea Island of the North Pacific") – with special Daddy Boats leaving Vancouver on Friday nights in summer to bring working fathers to the island for the weekend.

The Union Steamship Company died in 1959, a victim in part of the West Coast's expanding airline industry. One of the lines had been founded in 1943 by an itinerant radio repairman who grew up on Savary. Jim Spilsbury bought his first aircraft, a Waco biplane with wheels, skis, and floats, to better service the coastal customers he was seeing by boat. Suddenly he could travel places as far north as Hardwicke and Village islands as part of a trip that took seven and a half hours by air instead of a month on the water. Spilsbury's bush-flying company became Queen Charlotte Airlines (QCA). Some said the initials stood for "Queer Collection of Aircraft"; among the craft was the awkward-looking, Canadian-built Stranraer flying boat whose toilet was a rubber tube to the outside that whistled when open. Along with a scheduled service to the Charlottes, QCA's planes also stopped along the way at such resource-rich islands as Minstrel, Cormorant, and Broughton. As Spilsbury later reminisced in *The Accidental Airline*, "Of all the queer collection of aircraft we assembled in the course of our bargain-hunting, it is clear to me the one we'll be most remembered for is the gangling Stranraer, the 'whistling shithouses' we set beating their ungainly way up and down the fog-shrouded cliffs of the B.C. coast, loaded to the gunwales with Chinese second cooks and Finnish chokermen chewing snoose."

The people who come to live on the islands, full- or part-time, have always done so for intensely personal reasons that may be meaningless to others. These days, one common denominator in making such a decision is the apparent safety that the contained universes of islands can offer. Juanita

BIRD ISLAND

THEY GATHER AT SEA in the thousands, and at dusk, when predators are less of a threat, they start wheeling over the island in enormous circles: rhinoceros auklets – stout ocean-diving birds, their hooked little bills stuffed with as many as 15 skinny sandlance fish to feed their chicks. They come whipping over the one-room cabin where six men and women spend summers researching on aloof Triangle Island, well off northwestern Vancouver Island. "It's actually dangerous, there are so many birds," says seabird biologist Ian Jones. "A couple of people have taken a few hits."

Birds own this fog-cloaked, treeless smudge of rock, a rough triangle less than a kilometre square, which lies 45 kilometres northwest of Cape Scott. The outermost of the isolated, uninhabited Scott Islands, Triangle is by far the prime nesting site for British Columbia's seabirds. Twenty percent of the province's population arrives here between April and September: among them, pigeon guillemots, pelagic cormorants, common murres, black oystercatchers, glaucous-winged gulls, and tufted puffins, with their bright, triangular bills and straw-coloured, summer-only head tufts. There are about 52,000 of these puffins, the biggest colony on the coast below Alaska. Not to mention such predators as bald eagles and peregrine falcons, mice and voles, along with harbour seals and perhaps 800 Steller's sea lions blanketing the reefs of one of their four B.C. breeding grounds. But the seabirds are the most dominant species on Triangle – including

an estimated 84,000 rhinoceros auklets, the fish-foraging adults about 40 centimetres long, and their half-sized, plankton-eating relatives, the Cassin's auklets, who number about a million, or 40-plus percent of the planet's population.

Auklets are members of the *Alcidae* family, who frequent salt water and come ashore only to breed. The rhino auklets bear obvious white plumes on the side of the head and, during breeding season, the vertical knob on the bill that gives them their name. They nest in burrows high on the precipitous slopes, some of them behind the researchers' prefab cabin, and

with their shortish wings beating like mad, launch themselves down the side of the hills. "They sound like an air force jet going over," says Christine Atkins, a graduate biology student who has done voluntary research work on Triangle.

The researchers have included such keeners as a young woman who, Dr. Ian Jones told us, "has been here for four days and has slept for only a couple of hours – she's a real aficionado of the nocturnal birds and can't get enough of recording their calls on a digital audiotape recorder." Another enthusiast was Anne Vallee, a University of British Columbia master's student who in 1982 died in a fall here; her name now graces the provincial ecological reserve that encompasses Triangle (and which allows only scientific and educational visitors).

A documented midden (a refuse heap of shells and bones) suggests Native

THOMAS KITCHIN · FIRST LIGHT

A lone tufted puffin, one of thousands found on Triangle Island.

habitation in the past. In 1910, a lighthouse station began operating on Triangle; a hurricane toppled it two years later, and its replacement shut down in 1919 because the fog was often too thick for its light to penetrate. Researchers have been visiting the island since the 1940s when what was then the B.C. Provincial Museum did studies here. "Triangle is the only place where there are 13 species of breeding seabirds. It's the best on the coast, south of the Aleutian Islands," Dr. Fred Cook says. Holder of the Senior Research Chair in Wildlife Ecology at British Columbia's Simon Fraser University, he has launched a major study, led by Ian Jones, in cooperation with the Canadian Wildlife Service and the Natural Sciences and Engineering Research Council. The population-ecology project focuses on bird species vulnerable to environmental hazards such as oil spills or loss of food sources through changes in oceanographic conditions. "Seabirds are particularly valuable indicators of ocean productivity," Dr. Cook has written, "and management of seabird populations requires that we understand the reasons for population changes." The reasons might be overfishing by gillnetters, a slow buildup of toxic contaminants in the birds' bodies, or sudden oil spills, such as the one in 1988 when a barge off Washington State dumped 875,000 litres of fuel oil into the Pacific, killing seabirds along the Vancouver Island coast, with the odd globule washing up as far north as Triangle.

Auklets, tufted puffins, pigeon guillemots, and common murres were especially hard-hit by the 1988 oil spill. Biologists working on the project have attached stainless-steel bands to the birds' legs and collect samples to estimate how many of the species there are, whether they are breeding, and what their survival rate is. The work takes the researchers to neighbouring islands, on voyages in a Zodiac where they can have close encounters with minke and humpback whales and harbour porpoises, and seabirds such as red phalaropes and a species of shearwaters that breed on sub-Antarctic islands. During the day, when the birds are out on the water, "you don't even know Triangle Island is a seabird colony," Jones says. "It's quite quiet, other than for sparrows."

When the researchers aren't working, they are generally sleeping in tents or the 24-square-metre cabin that doubles as an office and living and dining rooms. They mostly rely on rain for water. Dinner might be fish caught on the island; other food and supplies come in by Coast Guard vessel and helicopters that may visit half a dozen times a summer.

The island comes alive at night, which means the biologists must do much of their research in darkness, illuminated by headlamps. Darkness isn't the only hazard: bald eagles will attack when someone gets too close to their nests. Between them and the swarms of swooping rhino auklets, it is no wonder the humans on Triangle have to keep ducking.

THOMAS KITCHIN • FIRST LIGHT

A red-billed parakeet auklet, seldom seen from land except when nesting.

Chase, a realtor on Savary, where her recreational-cottage business is brisk, says, "This recent growth is about wanting to be someplace else. People know they have to make a living in the city, but when relaxing they want a place that's very family-oriented and that's safe for the kids." Permanent islanders, especially women, often talk about how secure they feel walking at night, even on darkened roads illuminated only by flashlight. Yet islands can't provide pat solutions to all the issues that mainlanders might bring with them. As Juanita also points out, "A lot of people come to an island with problems and hope they'll be solved. But all your flaws become magnified. We sometimes know one another too well." And on small islands, it seems, familiarity can breed consent. A few years ago, the summer people on Savary were gossiping about how several couples among the tiny band of permanent residents had mixed and matched spouses. A newcomer down the strait on Hornby described for us how an old-timer clued her in to who's who among the children at a community event: "This child here, there's the biological parent – who's now with that one there. The second child is by those two there, but she's living with those people." (Melding families has a long history here: in 1895, one of the earliest settlers on neighbouring Lasqueti Island swapped his 20-year-old wife for the 53-year-old spouse of another resident, and the two new couples continued to live on the island for a while.)

Island life creates peculiar pressures on children, too: teenagers, in particular, can become bored by the lack of amenities and turn to vandalism – or worse – for something to do (not long ago, Saltspring Islanders raised $135,000 to build a drop-in centre after two teenagers high on acid died while trying to make their car fly). Teens often have to commute to high schools on larger islands and eventually leave home to go on to college or a wider choice of work. A daughter of Jeff King, publisher of the *Queen Charlotte Islands Observer*, went to a private school in Victoria to prepare her for university; in her high school class back home, she was one of only a couple of students who planned on higher education.

Then there are the summer people. Attitudes to them must inevitably be mixed: their very presence, their buying of local food and services, arts and crafts, help the residents to live as islanders year-round. Yet mainlanders can stretch an island's resources to seam-bursting lengths – and do that at a time when the weather, the land, the potential for pleasure are at their peak. In our travels, we talked to both, the permanent people and the part-timers, but if we had any bias, it was to let the residents tell their stories. One impossibly beautiful June afternoon on Hornby we picked up a hitchhiking Reina ("It means *Queen* in Spanish") LeBaron, whose parents had settled on the island two and a half decades before. They came, during a wave of

BOB HERGER

back-to-the-landers that swept over Hornby in the sixties, to farm organically and live in a handcrafted house that still has no electricity. The lanky, open, thoughtful 21-year-old, dressed entirely in clothes she'd scavenged from the Free Store at the island's progressive recycling centre, confessed her confusion about the summer people. She volunteered that they prop up the economy for three or four months a summer, while pointing out that they can play havoc with Hornby's predominantly rural way of life – on one weekend two summers before, about 1,800 rallying cyclists and other visitors had suddenly swollen the island's population more than fivefold to an estimated 8,000. "We call them tourists when we don't know them, but when they're our friends coming over, it's all right," she admitted.

"Independence and interdependence – both of these are heightened on an island," says Hornby's Janey Bennett. She adopts her formal architectural historian's guise to explain the phenomenon: "The very definition of the separateness of an island requires that one disengage from the feeling of being part of the flow of humanity – yet being in a little side pond of humanity requires that one interacts supportively with one's co-inhabitants." Or as Dr. Victor Andrucson, Texada Island's busy lone doctor, told us: "The isolation of islands is a figment of people's imagination. People are more isolated in the city than they are on an island."

Such a sense of involvement leads to direct action. Des Kennedy is a popular gardening writer *(Living Things We Love to Hate)* and TV personality who lives on nearby Denman Island. "On islands," he points out, "people have an immediate relationship to their environment. A large part of the difference being here is that people have not surrendered to the feeling that 'we can't have any say in our community.'" The day we met Des, he was under three weeks' house arrest, with an electronic monitor on his ankle limiting his time outdoors to three hours a day. He was one of two dozen Denmanites arrested while protesting the logging of old-growth forest in Clayoquot Sound off the west-central coast of Vancouver Island.

Clayoquot presents a classic example of how vulnerable the islands of the West Coast can be. Meares Island is the home of the Clayoquot and Ahousat peoples; ancestors of these Natives have been living in the village of Opitsaht (current population: 200) for more than 50 centuries. All but five percent of the island's 85 square kilometres is clothed in old-growth temperate rainforest, while its superb water supplies the Vancouver Island community of Tofino. In 1985, after hundreds of Natives and other demonstrators blocked loggers from operating on Meares for five months, the B.C. Court of Appeal banned logging there until the Natives' land claim was settled by the provincial Supreme Court. In the summer of 1993, about 10,000 Canadians, including New Democratic Party Member of Parliament

The rainforested Queen Charlotte Islands, says one photographer, are "rugged, beautiful, tempting – and deceptive."

Kayakers and powerboaters find inviting harbours as they thread through the Gulf Islands' sheltered network of waterways.

Svend Robinson – and such prominent foreigners as environmental lawyer Robert Kennedy Jr., son of the assassinated U.S. senator – came to a clearcut across Clayoquot Sound on Vancouver Island to stop logging and peacefully defy a court injunction. More than 850 have since been arrested, some serving up to 60-day jail sentences, others placed under house arrest. This overwhelming act of civil disobedience followed the B.C. government's announcement that it would protect one-third of the sound. Critics said that because half that land was already within national and provincial parks, the province was saving only an additional 18 percent of forestland. Late that year, however, it signed an interim agreement with chiefs representing the First Nations in Clayoquot Sound, which committed the two parties to manage the land jointly. Although logging would be allowed, other options under review include the possibility of declaring the islands tribal parks, off-limits to the timber companies. Protests continued throughout 1994, signalling once more that British Columbians, other Canadians, and interested onlookers in other countries consider the islands off Canada's West Coast a precious heritage worth preserving.

IT IS JUNE 21, the first morning of our 54th summer, and the thumb-sized hummingbird is back again, this time with a mate, the pair of them dive-bombing the foxglove off the deck. The heron awaiting us on our arrival two nights before, this bishop among birds, cruises in for an awkward-looking, long-legged landing in the shallows. Suddenly as motionless as we are, it watches for unsuspecting fish. Eventually the heron lumbers off, wings as widespread as a jumbo jet's; we christen it "747." In comparison, the spume-white gull acrobatting through the air a moment later seems as sleek as a Concorde. Shorebirds peck in the gravel, crows beachcomb. And the harbour seals are out there, by now an extended family of eight, a big one hauled out on a boulder while the others circle, their noses out of the water, out of joint. An eagle touches down on a nearby rock, eager to share a salmon breakfast from the same patch. Behind the seals, in a long line across the horizon, are their other competitors for food from the sea: men and women in fishing boats, their hungry nets spread so wide. For the moment, anyway, the two worlds coexist.

CHRIS CHEADLE

GUNTER MARX

THESE FRAGILE ISLES

I N OCTOBER 1993, Charlie Pearcy got a phone call asking him if he could spare a few days to work on St. George's Anglican Church, which was being rebuilt in Ganges on Saltspring Island. A master carpenter, Charlie is in his seventies. In his retirement he had been helping friends with their building projects in his home carpentry shop. "I came over and they promoted me immediately to chief sawyer and tripled my salary," he says. Six months later, Charlie was still coming to work every day, still getting paid in home-baked cookies and comradeship.

A mist-mantled view from Mount Maxwell Provincial Park, Saltspring Island.

Life on the Gulf Islands can be like that. People move in with plans to spend their days fishing and end up working as hard as they ever did, but for free. One full-time professional carpenter worked on St. George's, and carpenters, electricians, and drywallers were hired as needed. But the crew that volunteered day after day was made up of old guys like Charlie. Art Beaddie, who had been a butcher in Vancouver, and Marsh Antonelli, a forester, were also in their seventies. The younger ones – only in their sixties – were Alan Robertson, who retired as a draftsman with a Lower Mainland engineering firm, moved to Saltspring in 1990, and had a quadruple bypass in 1991; Mike Stacey, a farmer on the mainland, who became the operator of the island water taxi and enjoyed fixing and selling his collection of old diesel engines; and Colin Lawler, a semiretired civil engineer, who volunteered as the full-time project manager in return for an honorarium.

The boss was Barry Valentine. Formerly bishop of Winnipeg, he had agreed four years ago when he was 62 to be interim rector of St. George's for three months. Later the parishioners asked him to be their official rector. He planned to see the building through to its consecration in the fall of 1994, and to retire the following year. Pointing out that 90 percent of his parishioners attend church every Sunday, Barry Valentine said, "There is a bonding here. There is a feeling of beauty about this job."

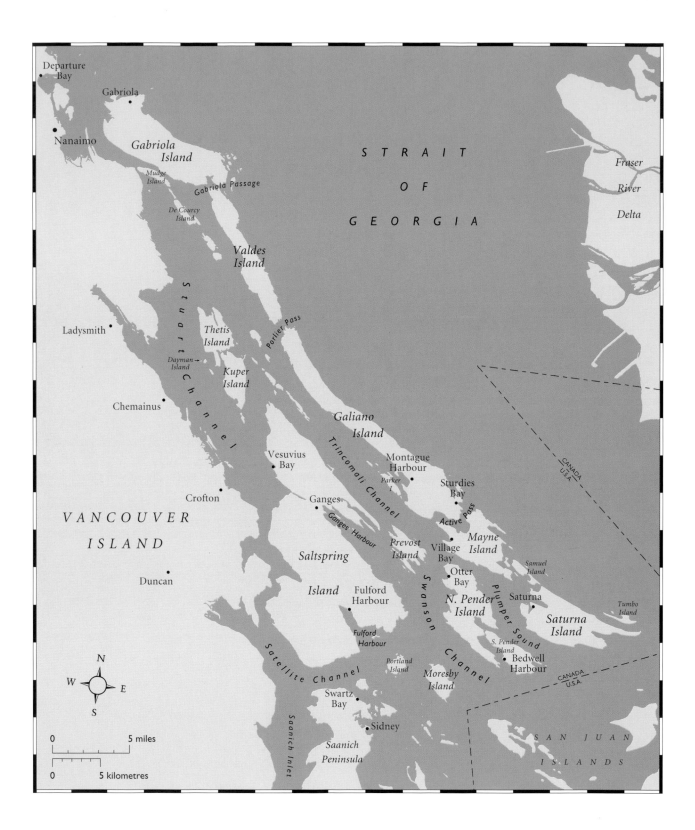

Departure Bay

Gabriola

Nanaimo

Gabriola Island

Mudge Island

Gabriola Passage

De Courcy Island

Valdes Island

STRAIT OF GEORGIA

Fraser River Delta

Ladysmith

Thetis Island

Stuart Channel

Porlier Pass

Dayman Island

Kuper Island

Chemainus

Galiano Island

Vesuvius Bay

Montague Harbour

Parker I.

Sturdies Bay

Trincomali Channel

Crofton

Ganges

Ganges Harbour

Active Pass

Mayne Island

Village Bay

Prevost Island

CANADA U.S.A.

VANCOUVER ISLAND

Duncan

Saltspring

Fulford Harbour

Island

Swanson Channel

Otter Bay

N. Pender Island

Plumper Sound

Saturna

Samuel Island

Saturna Island

Tumbo Island

Fulford Harbour

Portland Island

S. Pender Island

Bedwell Harbour

Satellite Channel

Moresby Island

CANADA U.S.A.

N
W E
S

Swartz Bay

Sidney

Saanich Peninsula

Saanich Inlet

SAN JUAN ISLANDS

0   5 miles

0   5 kilometres

ON A SATURDAY afternoon in early spring, a few cars line up for the four o'clock sailing to the mainland from Saltspring Island. The ferry terminal is quiet, for once a pleasant place to wait. Kids row a boat up Long Harbour in warm sunshine, and gulls skim cove waters looking for afternoon snacks. In several cars, city couples scan the real-estate ads in the *Gulf Islands Driftwood*. As summer nears, many more couples will come looking for a house or property. Among them will be people who see themselves living what developers' brochures routinely describe as an idyllic, easygoing life amid spectacular beauty and surrounded by friendly folk. The beauty and the bonding can be found on these islands, but life here has its own kind of stress – not just because of pollution, logging, and development, which may in the end transform the larger islands into suburbs with shores, but because the threat of loss hangs in the air. On islands the struggle against or *for* change pits neighbour against near neighbour, and the price of the struggle is often the tranquillity the islands seemed to promise.

This luscious archipelago is close to two densely populated and expensive cities. The pressure on the Gulf Islands to provide homes and cottages is intense. Newcomers seem to think the islands will stay as they were when they first discovered them. In the island phrase, they "pull their curtains" or become passive hangers-on. But island concerns have a way of pounding on one's door. A neighbour may decide to log, moving in noisy equipment; well water that once gushed may now trickle up; a developer may propose to turn the forest down the road into a city-style subdivision; rising assessments may inflate taxes beyond the means of retired people on fixed incomes. These issues wash onto the islands like the tides, spawning time-consuming controversy and divisive debate. It is no wonder that Saltspring islanders, relaxing at the Vesuvius Pub on a Friday night, smile in understanding at the middle-aged woman who raises her voice above the congenial hubbub: "The issues change and the bullshit goes on."

Island communities must decide matters that city dwellers long ago delegated to planners and politicians. In frequent public meetings, Gulf Islanders are invited to take part in the protracted process of revising the Official Community Plans that determine the size of building lots, the location of parks, and the type of allowable industry on each island. These plans must now be updated every five years. Under zoning set in previous community plans, the population of the islands, now at 16,000, would be allowed to double. Time and again people have told us that no one wants to lift the drawbridge, but the question today's islanders still debate is the one their predecessors also faced: how many people can these fragile islands support?

26

Bracketed by Nanaimo on the north and Victoria on the south, the Gulf Islands sit on the west side of the Strait of Georgia – 225 islands and islets. That they are called the Gulf Islands is the fault of Captain George Vancouver, who christened the strait the Gulf of Georgia. The resulting popular catchall term for the islands just wouldn't come unstuck, and in 1963 it was approved by the Geographic Board of Canada.

On a map, the larger Gulf Islands look like pieces of a geological jigsaw puzzle that could be nudged together and reattached to Vancouver Island. Saltspring, the largest, is closest to Vancouver Island. Out on the strait five islands form a breakwater facing the mainland 30 kilometres away. Gabriola is the archipelago's official northern limit. Tailing south from Gabriola are Valdes, Galiano, Mayne, and Saturna islands. West of this row, in Trincomali Channel, there are Thetis and Kuper islands, the east coast of Saltspring, and Prevost, which together make another north-to-south line, ending at North and South Pender islands. South of the main body of Saltspring, a scattering of small islands – Portland, Piers, Moresby, Coal, and Sidney – stops at D'Arcy, the official southwestern limit.

Eight of the islands have communities larger than 100 people. Some are privately owned (see page 9) and some are provincial parks or ecological reserves. Over the years smaller islands have been put to unfortunate uses. Piers Island was a jail for 600 Doukhobors sentenced in 1932 to three years' imprisonment for nudity in a public place. Boaters who visit the provincial park on D'Arcy and Little D'Arcy say they have been overwhelmed by sadness or haunted by the notion that they would never be able to leave. D'Arcy was a leper colony from 1890 to 1924, where as many as 21 lepers lived as outcasts, without nursing care, supplied only from time to time with food, opium for their pain, and caskets for their corpses. Because of the colony and its closeness to the Canada-U.S. border, D'Arcy was a favourite spot for smugglers to hide their booze.

The larger islands are linked to the mainland, Vancouver Island, and one another by car ferries, which ply routes so picturesque that repeated crossings cannot make them mundane. If they weren't primarily a means to move residents and cars to and from the islands, these voyages in attractive white ferries would be as romantic as cruises up Norwegian fjords. In fact, one world traveller and notorious romantic, Edward VIII, then the Prince of Wales, said the steamer voyage from Vancouver to Victoria "is the most beautiful trip of the kind in the world."

From the mainland, ferries leave Tsawwassen and cross the open strait for about 40 minutes before they are embraced by the islands. The entrance to Active Pass is marked by Mayne Island's Georgina Point Lighthouse, and from then on wooded, rocky shores and tiny, mossy islets slide by on either

Summer in the Magic Lake subdivision, North Pender Island.

BC Ferries' super-vessels often meet in the close quarters of the Gulfs' Active Pass.

side, sometimes within hailing distance. The ferries navigate the busy, sinuous pass like a skater on a bend, turning into emerald bays, where the unloading and reloading proceed in a pleasant ritual: the "walks-ons," with bundle buggies, wagons, or suitcases, walk off first and usually pause to talk to someone in the group gathered outside a portable waiting room. After the cars, campers, and trucks have bumped over the metal ramp and filed into the interior, more people with bundles and baggage trudge on board, followed by vehicles that have waited in orderly lanes. The ramp lifts. The ferry backs out and turns. So it goes at Galiano's Sturdies Bay, Mayne's Village Bay, and Pender's Otter Bay. Then comes the stately progression up Saltspring's narrow Long Harbour, observed from both shores by glassy-eyed houses cantilevered over rock or tucked in among trees where the Canadian flag flies.

In their primeval solitude, these islands were so densely forested that squirrels could cross them on overlapping tree branches. The islands remain part of the smallest of British Columbia's 14 biogeoclimatic families – the Coastal Douglas Fir Zone, which comprises only 0.3 percent of the land area of the province. In all of Canada there is no place more temperate: it does snow on the islands but the mean January temperature is three degrees Celsius. The zone has an almost Mediterranean climate, with sunny, dry summers and winter rains. The ubiquitous red cedar grows here, but this is where we find most of the province's rust-skinned arbutuses (the only broad-leaved evergreen native to Canada), broad-leaf maples that turn yellow in autumn, red alders, Douglas firs as straight as the columns of cathedrals and topped with pyramid-shaped crowns, and the astonishing Garry oak. Throughout the Gulf Islands, small complex ecosystems exist around lofty Garry oaks, which are the largest, longest-lived broad-leaved deciduous trees in Western Canada. Adapted to cyclical fires, Garry oaks survive on rapidly drained soils and steep slopes. In meadows under these majestic trees, blue camas, white Easter lilies, yellow western buttercups, chocolate lilies, and little monkey flowers bloom, and rare creatures such as the alligator lizard thrive.

In the 1850s, the islands waited, each with its treasures – the arable soil of Mayne, the fertile Fulford Valley and the copper and gold on Saltspring, the coal deposits on Tumbo, the sandstone quarries on Saturna and many other islands, the clay deposits on Sidney, the grouse and pheasant on Gabriola, and on all islands the towering trees that could be felled and shipped to world markets. They were inhabited or visited by Natives, whose shell middens testify to their presence as long ago as 6,000 years. Two bands of Cowichans, the Lamalcha and the Penelakut, lived on Kuper Island. Their fierce enemies were the Haida, who swept down from the Queen

AL HARVEY

29

Fall colours the vine maples that grace these islands.

30

THE POSSIBLE ISLAND

Bowen is Vancouver's possible island. Twenty-four kilometres northwest of Vancouver at the entrance to Howe Sound, this 32-square-kilometre island is the one that makes Vancouverites say, "We could live there." Young couples with children buy the houses they can't afford in Vancouver's middle-class neighbourhoods. Lawyers with practices in the city make the daily commute. Self-employed writers set up offices in Snug Cove and dash downtown to visit clients. Retired couples acquire forest trails and water views without giving up city pleasures and friends.

Residents of "the Republic of Bowen Island" can telephone toll-free to Vancouver. They can leave their downtown office at 4:50 p.m. and be on the beach with the kids before six. Twenty minutes of their trip will have been on an attractive new ferry, possibly sitting on the sunny upper deck chatting with neighbours. They can hunker down on the island and patronize the bakery (where you leave envelopes for Bowen Freight to deliver in the city), the general store (which is also the liquor outlet and unofficial bank), the delicatessen (cooked meats, fresh fish, and super soups), and Dunfield & Daughters (grains and beans in bulk, organic produce, and low-fat prepared foods). They can watch cable TV or have the Sunday *New York Times* delivered to their door. In an emergency, an ambulance will transport them onto the ferry and deliver them to a second ambulance waiting at the mainland terminal to whisk them away to hospital. Their kids will have lots of company and

a good education: the island has an excellent elementary school with a staff of 30 for its 320 youngsters. Students from grade 7 on can attend West Vancouver schools or an island private school for grades 7, 8, and 9.

Bowen's many possibilities are no secret. In the 10 years after 1976, the population doubled to 1,500. Over the next nine, it nearly doubled again. Another doubling would approach the maximum 7,000 that it is now estimated the island's resources can sustain. The flip side of popularity is pressure: house prices have risen so high that those young married couples with kids may

soon be excluded. Residents have been called upon to rework, discuss, and debate the Official Community Plan, dealing with such issues as the types of allowable industry, the nature of in-home occupations, and policies for the commercial village centre at Snug Cove (which offers books and videos, cappuccinos, and health foods). Water quantity is often an island problem. Quality is another matter: on Bowen, most people in Snug Cove gripe about the taste and smell of their water, which is from Grafton Lake, while residents of Queen Charlotte Heights on the island's east coast are looking for the best way to deal with the arsenic in their delicious well water.

But Bowen is still possible. Possible even for celebrity author Nick Bantock, who conceived the bestselling *Griffin & Sabine* at the Bowen Island post office

RUSS HEINL

("I was jealous about a person getting a nice piece of mail"). Bowen gave Bantock the privacy to write and illustrate *Sabine's Notebook, The Golden Mean,* and *The Egyptian Jukebox* and has spared him the soul-pocking adoration of fans. Somebody once asked a friend of Bantock if he knew that famous author on the island. The reply: "No, I know Nick Bantock, the soccer player."

Nick and his wife, artist Kim Kasasian, have been on Bowen since 1986. Freshly arrived from England, they took a day trip to an island they thought was called Bone. Coming into Snug Cove on the ferry, Nick observed, "This is stunning." His wife agreed. It took two months to become residents. Post-*Griffin & Sabine,* the Bantocks live with their four children in a house "with character" designed for and by them and situated in a meadow reminiscent of home in England.

The island allows Bantock to find a balance between the desire to be recognized and appreciated and the need to be left alone to work. What does he give in return? "My wife takes most of the weight." But he mentioned the soccer team he helped start and the craft sessions for his son's Cub Scout group. "What you give to the island is more about basic support and fondness for the place where you live. When you hear the ambulance, you wonder who it is. That's the notion of community to me. It's like a chosen family."

Bowen just gets more and more possible for financial planner J. Ross Allan, who has an office in downtown Vancouver to which he commutes three days a week, and a new office with a view in his house at Miller's Landing. Because of the need for confidentiality in a small community, he hesitated to pursue business on the island – until people began to request his services. "I could get into my jeans and do business down the street or get dressed in a suit and come into town." He's decided to do both.

For Ross and his wife, Suzanne, coming to the island in 1990 was a financial move; they wanted a house and some land and she wanted to be at home with Danielle, then six months old. Now, staying on the island is a lifestyle choice: this is where they want to raise their two daughters.

Ross has seen many young couples leave the island because they can't stand the commute, and understands the problems of travelling at peak times or when both parents commute. "The ferry sifts out those who can't live on an island," he says. Self-employed, he can catch the 8:30 a.m. ferry to Horseshoe Bay and "sail" over Lions Gate Bridge after the rush-hour traffic. Coming home, he leaves before 5:00 p.m. and arrives in time for the 5:25 sailing. As soon as he gets to Horseshoe Bay, he relaxes; by the time he's in Snug Cove, the stress of the day has washed away. While some commuters sit

in their cars and read, he chats up his neighbours. "I like the socializing. In the summer on the top deck in sunshine and short sleeves, we gloat about people in a sea of red lights going to Langley. Ours is a fixed commute. It doesn't matter when you go. It still takes an hour."

Edythe Hanen and her two adult children represent residents who have found a way to make a living on the island. They came here 20 years ago. Edythe is now business manager of the weekly *Bowen Island Undercurrent* (there's also a monthly magazine, the *Bowen Breeze*); her son has been employed on the island as a carpenter; her daughter as a cook at Doc Morgan's Inn. Edythe knew Bowen when it was inhabited by 300 hippies and old-timers, and remembers the potluck Thanksgiving dinners at Evergreen Hall. She lives in one of the 10 Orchard Cottages owned by the Greater Vancouver Regional District (GVRD) and all that remains of a summer resort that operated for 50 years in Snug Cove. Having interviewed and written about island pioneers, she is sad-

AL HARVEY

dened that history is being ignored by newcomers. "The island is invented the minute they come here," she says. Despite the loss of intimacy, she still feels supported by the community: "Even in casual friendships, I feel they are there for you."

Edythe has survived power failures (rare now that service has been improved); a frozen water pipe (thawing it with a hair dryer was "the biggest thrill of my life as a single mom"); a roof torn off in a windstorm (friends arrived in the early-morning dark with a large tarpaulin and later built a new roof without taking payment for their work); and an Achilles tendon torn after the last ferry had left at 9:45 p.m. (transported by water taxi and ambulance, she was at Lions Gate Hospital in half an hour). "There's no down side. I'm here because of the way it is. I'm not here to make it something else."

Inevitably Bowen will become something else. But, no matter how much the city encroaches, it will always be an island. For some, when the last ferry returns to the mainland and the island is dark and still, the mainland seems very far away indeed. For others who use the city but love their rural community, peace descends with the severing of that tie to the mainland. "Bowen," says Ross Allan, who stands with a foot on both shores, "is as far away as you imagine it to be."

Ferries not only make living on islands possible, they also act as mobile bulletin boards and social centres.

GUNTER MARX

34

Charlotte Islands. Battles were still being fought on the beaches of Saltspring when the first settlers arrived in 1857. They were 30 black Americans, who had bought their freedom from slavery and with determination made their way out of the United States. European settlers followed within two years, and the familiar process of settlement on preempted land began, extending to each of the larger islands within a dozen years.

In 1929, British writer Lukin Johnston travelled by steamer from Vancouver so that he could walk the gravelled roads of Mayne, the Penders, and Saltspring and meet the residents who he had been told were slightly "queer." Because Gulf Islanders tended to be so long-lived, he was able to talk to several octogenarians who had been among the first settlers and to three of the islands' most unconventional characters who had arrived later.

On Mayne, he met Colonel and Lady Constance Fawkes and Eustace and Grace Maude. At the time of his visit, the Fawkes were the owners of a 35-room mansion that sat near the Georgina Point Lighthouse at the eastern entrance to Active Pass. It had been the Point Comfort Hotel, a place of repose for travellers until 1900 when teetotalling Mrs. Maude had closed the bar. In their 20 years of residence, the Maudes failed to make repairs, simply moving to other portions of the building when plaster ceilings collapsed on them. Throughout this demolition by neglect, the Maudes continued to entertain at parties, and one guest remembers their quickly improvised solution to the minor inconvenience of a flooded dining room floor: their son George drilled holes into the wood so the water could run off.

Eustace Maude, a former first lieutenant on the royal yacht *Victoria and Albert* and retired Royal Navy commander, was 81 and in the final year of his life when Johnston met him. He told the writer he hadn't given up on the idea of sailing solo to England, a feat he had first attempted to worldwide attention at the age of 77. Heading for the Panama Canal, the commander reached Eureka, California, where in a storm he was hit on the head by the boom. Concussed and unable to see well enough to read his compass, he nevertheless found his way back to the Strait of Juan de Fuca and was towed to safety after 97 days at sea.

In 1924, the Maudes sold the crumbling Point Comfort house to Colonel and Lady Constance Fawkes, she being the daughter of the Marquis of Ailsa in Scotland. The Fawkes repaired the house and named it "Culzean" (*Ku-lane*) after the castle where Lady Fawkes had lived as a child. She spent her days on Mayne doing good works, making underwear for needy children, organizing a fall fair, and singing hymns on the wharf as the supply boat arrived. Lionel Grimston Fawkes, who had a reputation in England as an artist, was still happily painting on the island at the age of 70.

On Saltspring, Johnston called on "The Squire," a man described to him

Saltspring's landscape runs the gamut from the highest mountains in the Gulfs to the lilting farmland of the fruitful Fulford Valley.

as "queer but generous and good-hearted." British-born Henry Wright Bullock arrived on the island in 1892 as a young man. The wealthy son of a fellow of St. John's College, Oxford, he bought a huge property near Ganges and set about creating a country estate and model farm, where he threshed grain using a steam engine and generated electricity with a gasoline engine. He tried to improve the dress and manners of the locals, urging the young women to attain wasp waists and to wear shoes with stiletto heels. He gave women earrings if they would have their ears pierced, and supplied suits for young boys to wear to church. At lavish formal parties and seven-course, sherry-laced dinners, guests were served by liveried servants – boys rescued from London slums or an orphanage in Victoria. Bullock died on the island in 1946 when he was 79.

While the more populated islands tolerated and even sustained the slightly dotty, the private islands gave free rein to extreme characters such as Captain Horatio J. Robertson, who in 1887 bought Moresby, south of Saltspring, and built a house with two octagonal towers connected by a single-story, glass-fronted gallery. He, his wife, and three daughters used the one tower, while his eight sons occupied the other. Robertson liked to ride through the streets of Victoria in a rickshaw pulled by his Chinese servants, two of whom nearly died trying to escape from Moresby by boat.

Perhaps the most famous island owner was the charismatic, polygamous, and hornswoggling Brother Twelve, who set up a machine-gun-protected colony for his Aquarian Foundation on De Courcy Island. A sea captain named Edward Arthur Wilson, Brother Twelve (so-called because he was the 12th member of an occult brotherhood or, some said, the 12th great mind of the world) also built a mystery house on nearby Valdes Island, where he allegedly stored the fortune in gold he took with him when he disappeared in 1933.

Today, although the Gulf Islands are in the same biogeoclimatic family, the larger ones have become as different as cousins. Size and location seem to have created character, and in time, as people selected the places that suited them, the islands' personalities have been reinforced. There are now fabricated or imported similarities: each of the islands has an elementary school, churches, a volunteer fire department, stores, and a café, as well as a medical facility. Some have a golf course and country club, tennis courts, library, recycling depot, parks, and camping grounds.

Galiano is the most organized and inventive in its efforts to preserve its environment. The island is 25 kilometres long and only about two wide, with a single paved road connecting a community in the south to another in the north. Most of the 850 residents are in these two hamlets. In between them, MacMillan Bloedel (Mac Blo) used to own 3,156 hectares of forest (56

LIFE IN THE WILD

High above the sea, a couple of bald eagles cartwheel in courtship. In the past hour, we have spotted red-necked grebes, common loons, and a glaucous-winged gull on the rocks, regurgitating its gastric juices to digest a starfish too big for its gullet. Minutes before, we watched a mother seal with a pup on her back, swimming just off-shore in a sheltered training pool where the baby would learn to swim. Yet not far behind us, along this forested western flank of Galiano Island, houses on stilts hug tall bluffs. Less than an hour's ferry ride from British Columbia's thickly populated Lower Mainland, we are amid the Gulf Islands this spring day, on the bountiful waters of Trincomali Channel in the Strait of Georgia.

The skipper of our lemon-coloured catamaran lowers the sails as he tells us about a natural drama he witnessed very near here – a black turnstone cleverly eluding a relentless peregrine falcon. The little turnstone, one of the sandpiper family, is the commonest shorebird along the province's rocky coastline. The much rarer peregrine, about twice the size at 38 to 53 centimetres from tail to bill, may be the fastest raptor in the world. It can pounce on its prey at a velocity of 250 kilometres per hour (England's Naval Research Laboratory clocked one dive at 440 kilometres per hour). But in the skipper's story, strategy meant more than speed. Tom Hennessy says the fleeing turnstone had desperately flown beneath his catamaran, between its pontoons, which forced the startled falcon to slam on the brakes in mid-air.

Now we ease by abrupt cliffs pocked with holes – "bird condos," someone remarks – and up there atop a shabby fir perches a peregrine falcon. "That's a male. Nice grey back. The female is probably nesting or doing the washing up," says Graham Sunderland, the naturalist on board, narrating our tour with arid English wit. Pelagic (open-sea) cormorants, their plumage sleek and entirely black, share this cliffside colony with violet-green swallows, which feed on the flies buzzing about the guano that stains the rock like melted chalk. The swallows, with their characteristic white cheeks and flanks, hang out together in coastal flocks like this one to help each other spot and evade hawks and other predators. Sunderland points out surf scoters overhead, ducklike birds with distinctive fat bills of ebony, white, and reddish orange; the males as dark and lustrous as obsidian, with milky patches on the forehead and back of the neck. After a brief breeding season in the Arctic, they spend most of their time just off the Pacific seaboard, amid the islands. "There are hundreds of thousands of them all up the coast," Sunderland says. "They make no sound – you can see a flock of 20,000 and it will go by in silence. They make the occasional grunt on the breeding grounds – well, don't we all?"

With the noon sun burning through a silver sky, glancing off the quiet pewter sea, we tack toward the Balingall Islets, a couple of hiccups of rock on the way to Saltspring Island. The only foliage is a half-dozen twisted, skeletal trees – Rocky Mountain junipers that might be a century old. There, parked on twig nests, are double-crested cormorants, with their identifying dab of orange just beneath the bill. This is one of the few places anywhere (and the only site in British Columbia) where they nest in trees. Several of their smaller pelagic cousins are roosting around them on the stony ground.

The ubiquitous bald eagle.

The catamaran anchors on the protected lee side of nearby Parker Island. As we lunch on smoked salmon, fruit, and California wine, two belted kingfishers chatter along the gently slanting, log-littered shore, flashing their powder-blue backs and the blue-grey belts on their chests that give them their name. Two large Canada geese nesting on the point of the island flap by, low to the water, while above us a trio of red-crested turkey vultures circles patiently, languidly, casing the scene for carrion. All this action, while our skipper entertains us with a story about sighting a bald eagle in these waters clutching a huge salmon. Worried that the eagle might drown, he hopped in his dinghy to rescue it. But with the fish locked in its talons, the bird breaststroked to shore – where one of a pair of eagles scouting overhead swooped down and stole the salmon.

Given this dramatic setting, this richness of life in the accessible wild, it is little wonder that Hennessy honours the 26-year-old self who made a bold decision one day in 1971 during a visit to British Columbia. A city-bred American, born in the Queens borough of New York City and schooled in Washington, D.C., Hennessy was ignorant of the very existence of the Gulf Islands until that morning. Seeing a sign on the Vancouver side of the Strait of Georgia, he whimsically took the inter-island ferry to its first stop, Galiano, and instantly announced, "I want to live here."

The islands off British Columbia's mainland offer a front-row view of a show of natural pleasures that in their variety and abundance are unique in Canada. Beyond the cornucopia of sea and shore birds, waterfowl and raptors, there are such obvious marine mammals as harbour seals and sea lions. British Columbia is also host to several species of whales, including the orca, labelled a killer, and even sharks. Yet, like killer whales, the six-gilled and infrequent great white sharks have never been involved in a documented attack on a human here. On the populated islands between the Strait of Georgia and Hecate Strait, just south of the Alaskan Panhandle, the wildlife is equally benign. No poisonous snakes, no cougars, and no fearsome grizzlies – not even on the remotest reaches of the Queen Charlotte Islands (which *do* have Canada's biggest black bears). Oh, the odd cougar might swim over to an uninhabited island from the wildcats' prime habitat on Vancouver Island. There have been wolves on such islands as Cortes, Read, and Sonora, and a recent bear on Bowen. And while a handful of the exceptional white Kermode bears haunts Princess Royal Island south of Kitimat, they and their more plentiful black bear relatives display an unusual trust in humans. Botanically, too, these islands can be beneficent, husbanding uncommon if not outright rare flora, especially on the Charlottes and the salubrious Gulf Islands.

This bounty tends to attract lovers of nature to live on the islands. People like our skipper, a former industrial designer who with his wife, Ann, runs Sutil Lodge and a nature-tour business they call the Gulf Islands Institute. Their first day on Galiano, a quarter of a century ago, they watched salmon fishermen unloading their packers. "One of them gave us three salmon that were too small," Hennessy remembers. "We just camped on the beach for three days. We decided Galiano would be a fabulous place to raise children. The clear air, the view – everything hit me. It was like the most beautiful park I'd ever been in."

ESTHER SCHMIDT

The less-ubiquitous black bear.

percent of the island). The company's proposal in the late 1980s to divide the land into building lots split the community into factions. Attempts by the conservation-minded to pass zoning bylaws to restrict the use of the land to logging led to a court case that was decided in Mac Blo's favour. By 1994, the company had sold all but 111 hectares, most in large lots, averaging 48 hectares. In 1995, Galiano residents again went to court to try to prevent the new owners from subdividing their properties into eight-hectare residential lots. An island watcher calls proactive Galiano "the shining light" of the islands because so much land has been purchased by the community or secured in other ways for perpetual public use.

Although the island's southwest side drops sharply to the sea and much of the northeast is owned by people who bought from Mac Blo, there are a few public beaches on the southeast and at Coon Bay on the north. Receiving little summer rain and having only one small lake, Galiano is the driest of the southern Gulf Islands. Some residents in the south end store rainwater in plastic swimming pools, and because fire is a major threat, both communities have volunteer departments.

Mayne islanders say they act more independently than Galiano residents. An observer says they have no community political will and meet only when they have to. They seem not to like limitations on their personal freedoms: in the process of reviewing their community plan, the islanders turned down a bylaw that would have limited (not prohibited) foreshore development, such as docks, on private properties. Mayne is the smallest of the populated islands, with 835 people on 21 square kilometres. This was the first of them to have a post office, school, Anglican church, hotels, and a jail (Plumper Pass Lockup is now Mayne Museum). St. Mary Magdalene Church, founded in 1887, and Active Pass Lightstation (active since 1885) are tourist attractions. By the turn of the century, Vancouverites were visiting Mayne's lodges, hotels, and numerous pubs, which earned the island the nickname "Little Hell." Pioneer farmers raised sheep and grew King apples, which are still harvested; in the 1920s, tomatoes were successfully grown in a greenhouse large enough for a horse-drawn cultivator. Now Mayne has farms, a gently rolling landscape ideal for cycling, and many bays, public beaches, and inviting Dinner Bay Park, a picnic area created by community volunteers. Mayne islanders like to boast that, because they are the transfer terminal for Saturna, they have the best ferry service.

North and South Pender islands – originally one island joined by an isthmus – were separated in 1903 when the federal government cut a canal. They were linked again in 1956 when the provincial government built a bridge. In 1994, thrifty islanders were busy salvaging the timbers from that bridge for a community hall. An active resident says that the absence of a

GUNTER MARX

*Above: Catching up on the
outer islands' news.*

*Opposite: Mountainous
Saturna has only 280 residents,
but even they have faced
controversy over
land use.*

central meeting place (other than the school gym) is characteristic of a community that is hard to arouse to public action.

North Pender (2,685 hectares) has 1,400 residents, divided into two groups. Most live at Magic Lake Estates, one of the subdivisions with one-fifth-hectare lots that led to a government-proclaimed four-hectare freeze in the 1960s. There are now 700 houses on the 1,200 lots, about one in three being empty in the winter. The other islanders are living rural lifestyles on larger parcels of land. Many Magic Lakers who used to visit in the summer have now retired and live here permanently. In the past five years, there has been a 43 percent rise in water drawn from Magic Lake (while the number of wells has doubled in little more than a decade). North Pender is home base for *Island Tides*, a twice-monthly newspaper distributed free to the outer islands. South Pender (810 hectares) is more rural. Its 150 residents use the commercial and service facilities on the north island. Because it is close to the Canada-U.S. border, South Pender's Bedwell Harbour is the site of a Canada Customs office where American boaters report on their way into Canadian waters. The first regional park in the Gulf Islands, Mount Norman on South Pender, is 100 hectares of mixed woodland, old-growth forest, and sensitive ecosystems.

A resident of far-out Saturna (in the minds of many, the ferry transfer at Mayne puts the island farther away) describes his fellows as independent freethinkers whose method of organizing community events is "self-actuated ad hockery." Controversy is a latecomer to the 280 residents of the 31-square-kilometre island. Five years ago, residents said Saturna was a quiet place, where there were no Galiano-like issues and where the rate of logging on privately owned lands was slow enough that nobody was much bothered by it. Traditionally opposed to parks, the islanders had approved only one – at Winter Cove. But in 1994 they were aroused to alarm by the cutting of a wide swath of trees for a highway behind a *proposed* subdivision, and they fought among themselves over creating a park, which some residents suddenly wanted. The site in question was secluded Saturna Beach, a property owned by an islander who wanted to develop it into a 31-lot, water-access-only subdivision. The beach used to be the location of the famous July 1 barbecue, which attracted hundreds of boaters to eat local lamb (since 1989, the event has been held in Winter Cove Marine Park). Physically the island is mountainous, with five peaks and two nearly parallel mountain ridges running east to west. A 131-hectare ecological reserve perches on Mount Warburton Pike, and Environment Canada operates a station on Narvaez Bay Road where atmospheric and surface ozone layers are tested and air pollution is measured.

Saltspring is the most cosmopolitan of the Gulfs and large enough to

RUSS HEINL

offer city-style anonymity to its 9,000 residents and the occasional traffic jam in Ganges, its commercial centre. Saltspring is the official spelling, but residents adhere to "Salt Spring," to remind them of the name's source – springs of salt water near the north end, once described as "filthy holes that ooze rusty-coloured water." So far it is the only one of the islands with a hospital, secondary school, bus service, bank machine, and cinema (with a large screen and comfortable seats). From sushi to late-night jazz, Saltspring provides most things a city escapee may secretly want, as well as relative peace and trees. Because it is so close to Vancouver Island, many islanders commute from Fulford Harbour to Swartz Bay (35 minutes) en route to Victoria, or from Vesuvius to the Vancouver Island pulp mill town of Crofton (20 minutes). But because it is the last stop on the Long Harbour-Tsawwassen ferry, a door-to-door trip to Vancouver can exceed four hours. On its 185 square kilometres, Saltspring has seven lakes supplying potable water (although Maxwell Lake water requires chlorination, and algae are blooming on St. Mary and Cusheon lakes). One of its four mountains, 701-metre Bruce Peak, is the highest point in the islands, and Mount Maxwell is worth the hike for its expansive view of Fulford Harbour and beyond. The bountiful Fulford Valley, where pioneer farmers could fill two dozen 22.6-kilogram boxes from one apple tree, is still quintessentially rural.

Gabriola, 25 minutes from Vancouver Island, has a reputation as a bedroom community of Nanaimo. Nevertheless, many of its residents are retired. There are communities on the north and south ends of the 50-square-kilometre island. About 1,120 hectares of forest between the two are owned by Weldwood of Canada Limited, a logging company that has applied to develop 368 building parcels, with 720 hectares dedicated for community use. Northeast of Descanso Bay, where the ferry arrives, are the Malaspina Galleries, the island's fantastic natural attraction, explored and sketched in 1792 by the eponymous captains Galiano and Valdes. A wave-eroded sandstone cliff forms an arcade under which visitors can walk for about 100 metres. Gabriola's most enduring distraction – the Great Bridge Debate – is more than an engineer's fantasy. Bridging the narrows between Gabriola and Mudge Island and between Mudge and Vancouver Island is feasible. What many of the 2,500 permanent residents would regard as a tragedy, some – perhaps those who commute to Nanaimo – do support. Meanwhile, water and sewage are critical island problems. Residents are used to wells drying up in summer and have installed rainwater cisterns. The 1978 community plan outlined the danger to the water supply because the island's cover of soil wasn't sufficient for septic fields and because fractures of the underlying rock might allow seepage of effluent. Recently residents were reporting that their wells were pumping sulphurous goo, seawater, and fecal matter. For all its problems, Gabriola still boasts Silva Bay and its marinas, a favourite boaters' destination. The island also offers visitors petroglyphs, sandy beaches, several provincial parks, interesting marine life, and sandstone formations.

The Siamese twins, Thetis and Kuper, were joined near Telegraph Harbour until 1905 when the federal government dredged a canal and bridged it. Each island is about 26 square kilometres, and they are served by a small car ferry that runs frequently to and from Chemainus. With the last ferry leaving at 11:20 p.m. on Friday (stopping only at Thetis), the 250 Thetis islanders can take in a movie or symphony concert on Vancouver Island. Because of its closeness to the Island, Thetis is less self-contained than most other Gulfs. Residents shop in Chemainus, and it is easy to pick up a video there and ask someone to return it on the ferry the next day. The islanders have written into their newly revised community plan that Thetis is not to be regarded as a recreational destination. A resident said to us, "Put this in your book: Thetis has no crown land, no parks, no public facilities. There's

A skipper whips his powerboat through the breakers.

GRAHAM OSBORNE

nothing for visitors to do here, no store, no place to go for coffee." The community is strong in its desire to maintain the island's rural, tranquil, residential character.

With the exception of an eight-hectare farm that has been in one family for generations, Kuper is a First Nations reserve, the population of which is difficult to assess because many of the families move on and off the island. Across Porlier Pass from Thetis and Kuper is Valdes Island, which is not serviced by a ferry. Its only year-round residents live on one of the three First Nations reserves. MacMillan Bloedel owns 40 percent of the island, land that can be put to no other use than logging because it is part of the new Forest Land Reserve.

These islands, with the exception of Kuper (because it is a reserve), along with Lasqueti, Denman, Hornby, Gambier, and Bowen (see page 31), are governed by an elected body called the Islands Trust. Created in 1974 when the provincial New Democratic Party was first in power, the Trust is unique in Canada. Its herculean task was "to preserve and protect" the islands, their amenities, and their environment for the benefit of the residents and everybody else in the province. For many years, it was hampered by a lack of funds and a lack of authority.

In 1990, a new act revised the Trust, making it more autonomous. It could tax property owners and was given a broad land-use jurisdiction. It still shares authority with regional district boards, in charge of services such as water, sewage, and transportation, and with the Department of Highways, which approves subdivisions in the islands.

The 1990 act required the Trust to develop a policy statement saying how it would carry out its preserve-and-protect mandate. A "conservation-oriented" policy statement circulated for discussion in 1993 angered some islanders who feared that property values would drop or their land would be confiscated by the Trust. A milder, rewritten statement, signed into law in 1994, no longer obliges local Trust committees to restrain growth, nor protect forests, farmland, and environmentally sensitive areas. Now official community plans – which each of the 13 Trust areas must update every five years – have to "tend to implement" the Trust Council's protective policies or, if they would rather, set out their reasons for not doing so.

Opposed by contractors, developers, and some landowners, the Trust uses whatever tools it can to preserve and protect. One of its more imaginative and positive outgrowths is the Islands Trust Fund, a depository for land bought by or given to the Trust. The Fund is supposed to keep an inventory of unique features such as rare plants, animals, outstanding view locations, wetlands, and wildlife-rearing areas. While it can't compel landowners to preserve these features, the Trust Fund Board has persuasive

THOSE DEAR, FOUR-LEGGED DEFOLIANTS

THINK OF WILDLIFE on the Gulf Islands and the image that springs to mind, with the sudden speed of the animal itself, is that of a deer, especially the Columbian black-tailed deer, the so-called Coast deer, with their reddish-buff coats in summer, black noses and mouths, and white swatches on their necks, thighs, legs, and abdomens. The fur of the fawns is russet, dotted with white; the antlers of the adult males branch in two, which branch into two more. Semidwarf in size, bucks are often no more than 142 centimetres long and 68 high at the shoulders. Black-tails in the wild feed on shrubs, vines, leaves, lichens, berries, grasses, and clover. They are strong enough swimmers to move occasionally among the islands, where they can be found in the forests and open terrain as far north as the central B.C. coast. Sitka deer, a subspecies that looks virtually the same, range the northern islands, including the Queen Charlottes. And a relative few of a third type, fallow deer, are found amid the Gulfs.

There, deer are ubiquitous and sometimes troublesome – no more so than on a pair of islands in the southernmost Strait of Georgia. The problem of deer overpopulation has been most critical on James and Sidney, exquisite places only about 15 minutes by boat from Victoria, and privately owned except for provincially run Sidney Spit Provincial Marine Park. Speaking of black-tailed and fallow deer on Sidney, Doug Janz, a regional wildlife biologist for the B.C. Ministry of the Environment, says, "They're an exotic species, and they're tearing the hell out of the park." Accessible in summer by foot-passenger ferry from the town of Sidney on Vancouver Island, the park has open meadows, sable beaches, and a water-fowl-luring lagoon. Beginning in the late 1950s, a previous owner of 915-hectare Sidney Island installed peacocks, pheasants, wild turkeys, and North American black-tails. In recent years, while the birds died off, the deer population swelled to about 850, aided by the ancestors of fallow deer that swam the couple of kilometres from James Island (about a third the size of Sidney). Old World deer had been brought to James in 1908 from the Duke of Devonshire's estate in England to serve as quarry for members of the short-lived St. James Club. Between 1913 and 1978, James Island was home to a TNT plant; after it closed, an estimated 400 deer began denuding the island in a desperate search for food. James has since been groomed for a resort complex with a golf course and, although the island has no official hunting season, the deer numbers have dropped substantially. On Sidney Island, a logging syndicate responsible for planting tens of thousands of seedlings has allowed hunting and the transplanting of some deer to game-farming operations in the B.C. Interior.

"There are deer on virtually all of the southern Gulf Islands," says Janz, "and there are no natural predators other than man and his automobiles and his dogs. Nobody's really doing any counts on the islands." Except, he acknowledges, for a group on Denman led by local veterinarian Jennie Balke (see page 71), which has tallied an average of 120 black-tails, perhaps one-third of the island population. As well as hunters, and parasites such as ticks and lice, deer on inhabited islands are especially prey to dogs, which gang up to attack fawns and does. "They pull them apart," Balke says. "Deer aren't for running. They're for eating grass and wandering through the woods and hanging out – with little spurts of energy." When chased, they can suffer necrosis, in which stressed muscles die, causing the deer to succumb within a few days. To solve the problem on Denman, she and others called in a wildlife biologist to speak to the community – "and now we see people with dogs on leashes."

There are certainly enough of these elusive, solitary creatures that most islands have open seasons for hunters using shotguns and shot (Mayne and De Courcy are entirely off-limits and Bowen Island in Howe Sound allows only bow hunting). Denman's neighbour, Texada,

PAUL BAILEY

Black-tail deer, Denman Island.

has a season because this largest of the southern islands may have as many as 6,000 deer. Wildlife technician Mark Pimlott of B.C. Fish and Wildlife wonders "whether the currents through Malaspina Straits [between Texada and the mainland] are stronger than in other areas where predators like cougar, black bear, and coyotes have crossed wider bodies of water." Whatever the reason, the deer are abundant and so are the hunters. "In September, it's an absolute pain," says Bob Blackmere, who keeps a menagerie of animals on his Texada hobby farm. "You can have 400 bloody hunters crawling around here. One year they mistook a llama for a four-foot deer and shot it."

Urban visitors to most islands view resident deer as dewy-eyed creatures that reawaken childhood memories of Bambi; they are still startled to see such beauty on the hoof in their backyards.

Many islanders, especially the dedicated gardeners, consider the animals, as Balke jokes, "four-legged defoliants," super-efficient despoilers of every cultivated plant put lovingly into the soil. Their solutions to ward off the deer range from commercial repellents to creosote to lavender, from strips of Irish Spring soap hung on shrubs to human hair in muslin bags tied on perennials. Balke, who has worked with elephants in Africa, successfully tried lion dung from an Ontario zoo before deciding she didn't want to add to the deer's stress level.

The most effective deterrents are fences, although Pimlott cautions that "another frustrating factor about deer is that they are very good jumpers. So you're not going to keep them out with a 48-inch fence. You need up to a six-foot fence even with this quite small coastal deer." Balke first experimented with netting on poles, but "they busted down

every bit of fencing and one little baby buck ate all our lettuce and carrot tops and beans and peas." In frustration, she then graduated to a more potent electrical fence. Fellow Denmanites Des and Sandy Kennedy fenced in their rose arbour using 2.5-metre-tall cedar posts linked at the top by skinny horizontal rails and galvanized stucco wire strung a metre lower between the posts to preserve their view. But, in his book *Living Things We Love to Hate*, Des describes how two small fawns managed to slip through gaps in the split rails. "Once they'd squeezed through and begun feasting on our roses, their mother was frantic to join them. She'd try anything, including climbing the cedar rails, and knocking them down in her clumsy, splay-legged attempts. . . . I believe that in defensive strategies against these persistent marauders, 'almost perfect' is as close to perfection as you'll ever get."

FRED CHAPMAN

A fawn on Skungwai, Queen Charlottes.

tools, such as a 100 percent tax write-off for owners who donate their land to the Fund. Environmentally concerned owners can put covenants on their land to protect features such as trees.

Bob Andrew is a Saltspring Island trustee who entered politics by way of his position as the warden of an ecological reserve. "Trying to protect the land ends up in political action," he explained. Of Saltspring, he said, "We are trying to protect as much as possible, recognizing that it is too late for most of it." But mudflats and sandstone bluffs and parcels of forest aren't his only concern. The first problem he mentioned to us is affordable housing for longtime island residents. As retirees with pensions and well-off profession-al couples pay city prices for island homes, rising taxes and rents devastate islanders who have never had high incomes. "The shift has happened so quickly and it has caused agony on the island," he said. "There is a severe lack of housing and there is no infrastructure to take care of the problem."

Newcomers may be inconvenienced by a shortage of firewood or water, but Bob Andrew knows that such shortages are indicators of environmen-tal stress. "All the islands are growing at the fastest rate possible. One new family every day is moving onto this island. We are full – as indicated by the services, the ferries, and the lack of parking midweek in Ganges."

It is likely that those incoming moving vans contain a computer. Earning a living on the islands has become easier with a fax and modem and a few clients elsewhere in the bustling world. Those who must take jobs have limited choices, especially on the smaller islands where only so many waitresses, store clerks, and carpenters are needed (even those who, like Saltspring's Hopeless Construction Company, proclaim their services with the deprecating motto, "We don't claim to be perfect").

Commuting to Vancouver Island remains the favourite option. That has been Paul Minvielle's choice. He and his family fled the snowstorms of Montreal in 1976 and eventually bought a farm on Saltspring where they raised goats and chickens. While Loretta Minvielle worked as a nurse at the Lady Minto Hospital, Paul commuted to Victoria, first doing contract edit-ing for the provincial Hansard and later to work at the Victoria *Times-Colonist*. Now, with four children married and grandchildren on the way, Paul is planning for the day when he will retire from the *Times-Colonist*. Some years ago he and Loretta moved to an eight-hectare property off the Fulford-Ganges road. Paul's plan is to create a farm winery, modelled on the châteaux of his French ancestors, who came from Saint-Emilion.

Motorists stop and take pictures of the house he designed. The porte-cochère is grand enough to accommodate a horse-drawn carriage. And there is a tower ("every château needs a tower"), four stories high, with narrow windows ascending to a conical cap of a roof, from which tiny dormers face

CHRIS CHEADLE

Above: Life is one big beach at Port Browning, Pender Island.

Opposite: Flocks of sheep are routine obstacles on Saltspring Island's rural roads.

in four directions. The crest on the front of the house is a copy of the ring an ancestor brought from France during the Revolution. With 1,800 metres of drainage pipe in place and five hectares fenced against the deer, Paul will plant French hybrid grapes, and in a few years there will be a vintage for sale. Eventually he'll stop supplying eggs to his co-workers at the *Times-Colonist* and become the full-time seigneur of Château Minvielle.

Paul's lateral step into entrepreneurship is typical of islanders who convert hobbies to businesses, such as the bed-and-breakfast operator who bred and sold lovebirds, parakeets, African grey parrots, and Himalayan cats. Islanders encourage cottage industrialists – the picture framers, potters, and jewellery makers whose signs (made by a cottage industry) dot island roads. Many of the self-employed put out no signs: the islands' famous writers and painters (Saltspring wildlife artist Robert Bateman and poet Phyllis Webb; Galiano authors Audrey Thomas and Jane Rule; North Pender thriller writer William Deverell) are granted a life-preserving anonymity, except when they emerge to take part in the Gulf Islands Poetry Festival or to sign books at Volume II in Ganges, the only true bookstore on any of the islands.

49

*North Pender's shoreline,
indented with tranquil
coves and bays.*

The most common cottage industry is the popular bed-and-breakfast (49 on Saltspring at last count). Excellent inns and resorts, such as Hastings House and Oceanwood Country Inn on Mayne, which is listed in *The Best Places to Kiss in the Northwest* and *America's Best Little Inns and Hotels*, have made the islands year-round tourist destinations. Marilyn and Jonathan Chilvers, who conceived and own Oceanwood, might be said to be living a dream, but it wasn't *their* dream. Both of them were perfectly happy with their life in Vancouver where Jonathan had worked for McKim Advertising for 25 years and Marilyn was in a public relations partnership, with clients such as Canadian Airlines. They had been Mayne Island weekenders for several years when they saw a house for sale on Navy Channel and imagined it as an eight-room inn. Now innkeepers for 10 months of the year, the Chilvers are a fixture of the island economy. In 1994, they paid income to 18 people – a salaried chef and an assistant who has a guaranteed part-time income, and dishwashers, cleaners, and gardeners, paid on an hourly basis. After the 1995 winter break, Oceanwood reopened with seven new guest rooms, a testament to its success. The Chilverses' happy life on the island is by no means insular. As Jonathan told us, "I don't feel the world is passing us by. The world comes to us in the form of interesting guests."

As does the natural world to most islanders. Stephen Hume is a poet and a columnist for the *Vancouver Sun*. As a telecommuter, he could live virtually anywhere in British Columbia, and so chose Saturna, one of the least-populated Gulf Islands, "along the crumpled western edge of Canada." He tells how, in the summer of 1994, harbour seals with young pups panicked just off his beach as a pod of killer whales moved in. When one three-day-old pup wound up the next morning alone, wedged in nearby rocks, he worried about its fate. "It was alive," he recalls, "but it would shortly have its eyes pecked out by ravens." What else was there to do but call the local float-plane company to tote the orphan to the Vancouver Aquarium on a mercy flight? Harbour Air was happy to oblige but couldn't be in the area until the next day. What else to do then but put the baby seal in a cat cage, load it in his car, catch the ferry to the mainland, and deliver the ripe-smelling pup directly to the aquarium?

As EDMONTON LAWYERS or Saskatchewan farmers prepare to emigrate to the Gulf Islands, they are inevitably asked, "But what are you going to *do* there?" Newcomers with a smidgen of community spirit find the problem resolves itself; islands have a way of making use of new blood – as the congregation of St. George's Church discovered.

The building of the church in Ganges is an archetypical island story.

Wherever possible, local resources were used: a Saltspring company moved the original 1940s church across Park Drive and set it down on a rise above Ganges Harbour; cedar and fir trees, logged from the rector's property, were milled locally and used as roof beams and decking and as vertical lining boards at the main entrance; the $700,000 budget was raised mostly on the island and some finishing of the interior woodwork was done by people of other island churches, including a Roman Catholic priest who quipped, "I've come to put a stain on the Anglican church."

We visited in the spring of 1994 when the building was ready for temporary occupancy. Mike Stacey told us how he'd graded the property with Petunia, his 1929 tractor, and how 30 volunteers had turned out for the difficult job of stripping the concrete forms. He explained how the old 325-square-metre church had been incorporated into the new 855-square-metre structure. Standing in the nave, he looked up at the roof that now spans the original church and the added-on side aisles. "Us old guys built the trusses in here," he said. It was just a statement of fact, but we heard his pride and even astonishment at what they had accomplished.

It occurred to us that the island had given these old guys a nearly vanished opportunity – to build with their own hands a public building that will endure, a building their grandchildren will show to *their* grandchildren. We agreed with their rector that the people who have chosen to live on the Gulf Islands are special. It isn't cheaper land that draws them. Nor is it just a small community that they want. They have come because they are intrigued by the idea of life on an island, with all that implies about limited resources and self-reliance and, yes, caring for one another and future generations.

T.W.'S IMAGE NETWORK · CAMERON HERYET

BOB HERGER

54

FRAGMENTS OF THE PAST

THE RED-AND-WHITE de Havilland Twin Otter swung low over the island, over the long, wide beach of shimmering white sand, a tropics-like strand reaching into the warm shallows of the sea. Waiting on the summer shore were three dozen chitchatting women and frolicking children, most of them in bathing suits and bare feet. It was Friday evening on Savary Island and the Daddy Plane was landing. Delivering its weekend load of husbands and fathers from workaday Vancouver, an hour south along the Strait of Georgia. On the water now, its propellers growling, the 16-passenger Harbour Air floatplane backed up on to the beach. The Daddies emerged, in shorts or rolled-up suit pants, some of them pulling shore slippers from their briefcases, others shoeless and sockless as they waded through the surf. Smiling, they gave their families one-armed hugs while a human chain passed out the bags from the luggage compartment. After the Twin Otter took off, the only sounds were squealing kids and an Irish setter yelping in the water.

Two islands south of Savary, a small open-decked, three-storied BC Ferries vessel manoeuvred into a wharf on the rocky shoreline of Blubber Bay. Above the terminal, on a site once reserved for slaughtering whales, loomed a truncated mountain of dusty white limestone. An intricate network of conveyer belts brought the rock down to a Seaspan barge, its aft half-sunken with the weight. On the other side of the wharf waited the tugboat *Jervis Crown*. Texada Island was unloading some of the minerals that have made it rich. As cars and foot passengers disembarked from the ferry, the clatter from the loading dock was endless.

Separated only by flat-topped, uninhabited Harwood Island, Texada and Savary are as different as chalk and cheese. Or, in this case, lime and sand. The one is an industrial island, nicknamed the Rock, at 287 square kilometres the largest in the southern Inside Passage. Iron, gold, and copper – and the limestone used in making cement, pulp, and Rolaids – have fuelled Texada's economy for a century (along with illegal liquor and, more

At anchor, Khutzeymuteen Inlet, southeast of Somerville Island, the upper Inside Passage.

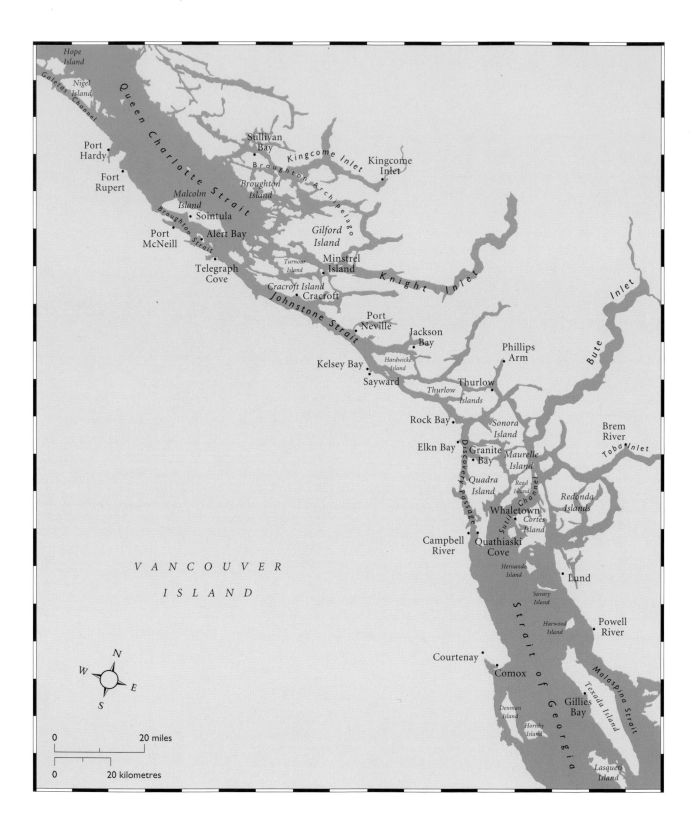

Hope
Island

Nigel
Island

Galeras Channel

Queen Charlotte Strait

Port
Hardy

Fort
Rupert

Sullivan
Bay

Broughton Archipelago

Kingcome
Inlet

Kingcome Inlet

*Malcolm
Island*

*Broughton
Island*

Sointula

Broughton Strait

Alert Bay

Port
McNeill

*Gilford
Island*

Telegraph
Cove

*Turnour
Island*

Minstrel
Island

Cracroft Island

Cracroft

Knight Inlet

Johnstone Strait

Port
Neville

Jackson
Bay

Phillips
Arm

Kelsey Bay

*Hardwicke
Island*

Thurlow

*Thurlow
Islands*

Sayward

Bute Inlet

Rock Bay

*Sonora
Island*

Brem
River

Elkn Bay

Discovery Passage

Granite
Bay

*Maurelle
Island*

Toba Inlet

*Quadra
Island*

*Read
Island*

*Redonda
Islands*

Sutil Channel

Whaletown

*Cortes
Island*

Campbell
River

Quathiaski
Cove

*Hernando
Island*

Lund

VANCOUVER

ISLAND

*Savary
Island*

*Harwood
Island*

Powell
River

Courtenay

Comox

Strait of Georgia

Malaspina Strait

Texada Island

Gillies
Bay

*Denman
Island*

*Hornby
Island*

*Lasqueti
Island*

N
W   E
S

0   20 miles

0   20 kilometres

recently, marijuana). The other is a classic summer isle; in spite of fitful, long-abandoned logging operations, Savary has been a dedicated holiday destination for Vancouverites, which as early as 1910 was billing itself as "Western Canada's King of Beaches." If Texada is Treasure Island, Savary is Pleasure Island.

Texada (population: 1,200) actually has one of its pleasant residential districts illuminated with streetlights; Savary (population: 50) still doesn't have – and mostly doesn't want to have – any hydroelectric power any-where. Texada has more daily BC Ferries sailings from the mainland than the Gulf Islands do; Savary continues to depend on the small inboard motorboats that make up a limited, private water-taxi service. An August issue of Texada's slick monthly *Grapevine* might publish a cable TV guide and a schedule for the Powell River transit system that intermittently serves the island; a late-June edition of the mimeographed *Savary Island News,* which takes the summer off, might have the lineup for theme nights at the Mad Hatter restaurant and ads for the island's three massage therapists. In their distinctions, Texada and Savary typify two extremes of those umpteen islands, north of the Gulfs, that are scattered along the Inside Passage.

THROUGHOUT THE INSIDE PASSAGE, that immense north-south waterway off the British Columbia mainland, there are fishing and logging towns, a few isolated Native hamlets and abandoned fish camps, mostly unmanned lighthouses, and the broken bones of long-ago boats. Lonely vessels thread through what is really not one marine highway but an unknowable labyrinth of large and small channels. Most common are fish-ing boats seeking crab, herring, halibut, cod, sole, red snapper, and five species of salmon. Other workhorses navigate these waters: tugboats tow-ing rafts of logs, or barges topped by loading cranes; local ferries scooting across the channels; large BC Ferries vessels carrying cars and passengers; sometimes canoes and kayaks, sailboats and other pleasure craft – little cousins to the summer fleet of 20 or more cruise ships between Vancouver and Alaska.

Here in channels carved by glaciers are the sea in all her humours, the infinite armada of unfrequented islets, the fretwork of steep-sided fjords, and the rain-forested flanks of the sky-poking Coast Mountains. Some summer days, the mountains wear what looks, from a distance, like a plush fur, in hues that run from lime-green through emerald to ebony. On a poster-ready afternoon, the hillocks of waves wink in the sun as if a million diamonds had been cast upon the waters, every diadem glinting in the light. The day, the scene, should be patented. Even someone as eloquent as the

58

pioneering American naturalist John Muir was at a loss for words in reporting his trip through the passage in 1879: "Day after day, we seemed to float in a true fairyland, each succeeding view seeming more and more beautiful. . . . Never before this had I been embosomed in scenery so hopelessly beyond description."

Today, amid the passage, there are islands like East Thurlow and Minstrel that bear only remnants of their mining, logging, and fish-canning pasts. In the late 1800s, Shoal Bay on East Thurlow had an estimated population of 5,000 loggers and gold-seekers, which made it larger than Vancouver, 200 kilometres south. And for more than half of the 20th century, although the mines and sawmill closed, the island remained a key refuelling and supply centre for boats, floatplanes, and helicopters. Now the only reminders of East Thurlow's history are crumbling log cabins and yawning mine shafts in the woods, and a government dock and a lodge in Shoal Bay. Minstrel Island, farther north at the entrance to Knight Inlet, was once as colourful as its name. It was apparently christened for a black-face minstrel show that accompanied Lord Dufferin, a Canadian governor general, on a voyage to a Native village in 1876. In the early 1900s, about 60 logging operations were harvesting the thick stands of enormous Douglas fir on Minstrel and the surrounding islands. Minstrel had a hotel saloon that could attract 500 loggers at a time, downing more beer than in any other lounge in British Columbia. For decades, the island maintained its rowdy reputation, one that logging poet Pete Trower experienced firsthand and recorded recently in his novel, *Grogan's Café*. In the 1960s, a drunken logging company owner bought the Minstrel Island Hotel after the manager cut him off. The man he sold out to a decade later was facing a court appearance one day in 1981 when he took off from Minstrel in his floatplane – never to be seen again, despite one of British Columbia's most extensive searches.

The passage has a few islands that are privately owned by a syndicate or an exotic foreigner and used solely for recreation – such as an intriguing trio just north of Savary: Hernando and the Twin Islands. Hernando was owned in the 1960s by Lake Tahoe developers from Palo Alto, California, who had unrealistic plans for a 3,700-unit resort, two marinas, a jet airstrip, and at least one golf course. "But they soon realized they were about 100 years ahead of their time," says realtor John Yuill, an island specialist with Colliers Macaulay Nicolls in Vancouver. In 1971, he handled the $1.15 million sale of the island to a group of buyers whose nucleus of 10 already had properties on Savary. At 1,040 hectares, Hernando was, at the time, the largest island along the coast under single ownership. The 50 shareholders included a few Americans and some people from Ontario, but most were high-profile Vancouver business and professional types (among them real-estate developer George Reifel Jr.

Paddling the crystalline waters at Whaletown, Cortes Island.

and Senator John Nichol). Hernando, which has rugged hills, sand cliffs, and some pretty beaches, maintains its rustic ambience despite stunningly designed homes and a tennis court. Architectural engineer Bogue Babicki's glass-walled house sits like a suspended spaceship above an oyster-rich reef that is a 25-minute walk from any neighbour. The owners allow only exterior stains, not paint; forbid any reflective surfaces but glass; and for a long time prohibited noisy diesel generators, so their lamps had to be lit by kerosene. When Austin Taylor, chairman of the McLeod Young Weir investment firm, contravened regulations and built a concrete causeway for his boat, the other islanders had it bulldozed.

Immediately north of Hernando lie the Twin Islands, also known as the Ulloas, which are linked by land at low tide. Since 1961, their owner has been Max Markgraf von Baden of Baden-Baden, Germany, whose mother was one of Prince Philip's four sisters. A decade later, the royal yacht *Britannia* anchored off the 80-hectare islands and the prince, Queen Elizabeth II, and Princess Anne spent a sun-drenched day salmon fishing, hiking, and having an outdoor barbecue. And before the royal couple's 1994 visit to the Commonwealth Games in Victoria, it was on the Twins that they took a day off. Caretakers Paul and Maggie Knepperges, who come from a heavily industrial area near Cologne, love the reclusive life they lead in an attractive cabin on a heavily treed waterfront estate. "Here the air is clean and there are beautiful wide-open spaces," says Paul, a former commercial pilot. He's nearing 60, she's in her mid-forties. They live next door to the main lodge, a massive log structure with seven bedrooms and five bathrooms, a huge rock fireplace, and an arbutus tree thrusting through the deck of the master bedroom. Once a week, they make a 25-minute speedboat run to shop in Lund, the last stop on the mainland highway north. A large garden and fruit trees help feed them year-round, and they get their power from generators and a water wheel in a small lake a kilometre away, which also supplies their running water. Their duties include trimming the lawn and clearing the old logging roads of fallen timber. Once, when Paul had a logging accident, a helicopter from Campbell River on Vancouver Island arrived less than half an hour later to take him to hospital. The owner's visits to the island are rare and brief. Seldom lonely, the Kneppergeses visit back and forth with other caretakers, like the young couple next door on Hernando. During our telephone interview, when we asked what they dislike about living on the Twin Islands, Maggie retorted: "Being bothered by phone calls."

And then there are those islands along the Inside Passage that combine competing attributes, retreats where people attempt to carve out a basic living in sylvan surroundings, at least physically removed from big-city ills.

THE TURBULENT HISTORY OF AN ISLAND OF HARMONY

YOU MIGHT EXPECT the first ferry trip of the day between Alert Bay, on Cormorant Island, and Port McNeill, on the northern tip of Vancouver Island, to be a quiet sort of milk run: just a few half-asleep islanders clutching Styrofoam cups of coffee, or ambitious tourists trying to get back to Victoria by midday. In fact, it is more like being caught in the bleachers during an inner-city basketball game. This is the boat that drops off hundreds of adolescents at the only high school in the area, and they spend the trip jumping over the seats, sharing cigarettes outside, and yelling to each other from deck to deck. Before the ferry discharges the excited students at Port McNeill – much to the relief of BC Ferries employees, who twice a day become reluctant hall monitors – it docks briefly at Malcolm Island, in a community called Sointula where a few dozen young foot passengers come on board. Unlike the kids from Alert Bay, most of whom are Native, the new arrivals are blond and blue-eyed, and they have names like Kiiskila, Pakkala, and Tynjala.

They are the descendants of a group of Finnish anarchists who came to Malcolm Island from Nanaimo in 1902, participants in an ambitious plan to establish an idealistic Utopia on a Pacific island, far from the city and the exploitation of bureaucrats and mine owners. Standing on the ferry dock at Malcolm today, it is obvious that Sointula never became the capital of a vast anarchist confederacy. In many ways, this town of 1,000 resembles other West Coast communities: it has one post office and one hotel; it is still too small to need a high school, and just large enough to support a sewer. Gillnetters and trollers bob behind a breakwater, logging trucks plunge down twisting roads, and Winnebagoes with American licence plates lumber toward fishing lodges on the fog-bound beaches of its south coast.

But it is also obvious that Sointula differs from other coastal towns. The streets here have no names, the houses are built on old-growth cedar logs that stir and then float as the tide comes in, and people still leave their keys in their pickups and their houses unlocked. Coming from Alert Bay or Port McNeill, you feel as though you've switched oceans: the solidly built houses with attendant saunas, the whitewashed co-op, and the overgrown, turn-of-the-century farmhouses all look like they belong to a cove in Brittany or a fjord in Norway.

The founding of Sointula – and the tragic dissolution of the original settlement – is among the most fascinating pioneer stories on the coast. While other towns were built around the promise of a railway or the proximity of a coal mine, Sointula was built around an idea – the particularly Utopian idea of a Finnish journalist called Matti Kurikka. While in his thirties, Kurikka had gained recognition as a leader of the Finnish working-class movement. Convinced that the salvation of the Finns lay in emigration, he wanted to found a colony in which "a high, cultural life of freedom would be built, away from priests who have defiled the high morals of Christianity, away from churches that destroy peace, away from all the evils of the outside world."

He came at the call of a group of Finns in Nanaimo, on Vancouver Island, disgusted with the conditions in the mines run by James Dunsmuir (who was also the premier of British Columbia). They were confident that if anyone could create a Utopia, it was this flamboyant speaker and pamphleteer. In 1901, when Kurikka and a small band of Finns sailed up the coast, 20-kilometre-long Malcolm Island was still uninhabited. Apart from the ruins of an English and Irish religious settlement, and middens left behind by

SHANE SCOTT

the Kwakwaka'wakw Natives who came to gather clams on its beaches, the island was untouched and undeveloped.

Although Kurikka had boasted to provincial authorities that "the use of the axe, saw, and knife are familiar to [the Finns] from childhood," he had neglected to mention that most of the Finns in Canada were craftspeople, farmers, scholars, and writers. After dubbing the new colony "Sointula" – the place of harmony – they set about trying to transform a damp, heavily wooded island without a sheltered harbour into something resembling a Utopia. While tailors, cobblers, and farmers were still trying to figure out how to cut down thousand-year-old cedars with handsaws, Kurikka was off plugging the benefits of the colony in New York meeting halls. Editions of the *Province* from 1902 tell of Finns from all over the continent arriving in Vancouver almost every week, sometimes by the boatload, most of them responding to Kurikka's glowing portrayal of a full-fledged Utopia on a Pacific island. He came back to Sointula after eight months to find the settlers still living in tents.

A disaster in January 1903 shook the settlers' morale. Kurikka, back from one of his regular trips to Vancouver to get credit from wholesalers, called a meeting in the three-story communal apartment house that was the only shelter for many of the settlers. With the entire community gathered on the top floor to hear about his trip to the city, a fire, caused by heating pipes that were too close to the cedar walls, ravaged the building. The headlines in the *Province* the next day told the story: "Eleven Burned to Death at the Finnish Colony – People Jumped from Third-Story Windows and Were Frightfully Hurt – Children Were Dropped into Outspread Arms Below – Those Who

Were Consumed in the Burning Building Comprised Eight Little Children, Two Women and One Man."

Kurikka was not gifted with tact. After ruining the colony with his forays into the city to get credit, and only barely surviving accusations that he had set the fire himself to destroy the colony's account books, he started aggressively campaigning for free love by attacking married couples in the pages of Sointula's internationally distributed newspaper. He went head to head with one of the colony's more practical-minded leaders, but it was Kurikka's head that fell. He departed, managing to take half the colony's population with him – most of Sointula's bachelors. Having decided that it was women who had queered his Utopia, he created an all-male commune in Websters Corners (present-day Maple Ridge, British Columbia). It lasted five months: while Kurikka was out of town lecturing, his comrades picked up some girls in the Fraser Valley. Disgusted with these "enthusiastic materialists," Kurikka left for Finland in 1906, and spent the rest of his life trying to convince people to come with him to India or New England to create a New Sointula.

But the old Sointula never died. The land was divided up into lots, and the island started looking something like a farming community on the Atlantic coast. The residents of Sointula founded a cooperative in 1909 (today it is the longest continuously running co-op in Canada) and started shipping cartons of eggs out to other communities. Some of the settlers farmed to provide food for their tables, and made a living through logging and fishing, taking tiny flat-bottomed skiffs out to Rivers Inlet in the days when each sockeye would bring a fisherman 15 cents.

Free love and communal property

might not have outlasted Kurikka's brief tenure, but Sointula had been founded by strong-minded men and women who were dead-set against authority, wage slavery, and organized religion. Signs of Sointula's radical past can still be found in its museum, a one-room building that was once the community's school. The photos on the wall are of Lenin and Trotsky, and the bookshelves include *The Handbook for Volunteers of the IRA, Notes on Guerrilla Warfare,* and *The Communist International, Jubilee Edition.*

If Kurikka left any kind of legacy to the citizens of Sointula, it is a fierce sense of independence. Starting in 1917, Malcolm Island fishermen led some of the most virulent strikes on the coast against the fish packers, often emerging as leaders. Even today, longtime residents say Sointula will never become a town; and if any newcomer is tactless enough to point out the advantages of incorporation, he'll be shouted down at the co-op meetings. Helen Tanner, a longtime resident, sums up a still-prevalent suspicion of institutions the outside world takes for granted: "Right up until the sixties, there wasn't a church, there wasn't a beer parlour, and there wasn't a policeman on the island. You had to dole out your own punishment." What sets Sointula apart for Helen is *attitude.* "Sointula was built up with volunteer work. The Finnish Organization Hall and the store were both built by volunteer labour. A few years ago, I happened to be on the school board with a lady from Alert Bay. When I told her we did the painting as volunteer labour, she said: 'In Alert Bay, we have to pay for *everything.*' The same with shingling a roof or fixing a boat. Your neighbours are always volunteering to help you. In Sointula, you aren't doling out the almighty dollar all the time."

Among them (south of Texada) are Lasqueti, and (above East Thurlow) Malcolm Island, where turn-of-the-century Finnish political refugees founded a utopian settlement in Sointula, now a fishing and arts community (see page 61). Another attempt at Utopia began in 1967, when Ted Sideras and a business colleague from Oregon formed a commune on 32 raw hectares of Lasqueti (and later on Calvert Island, north of Vancouver Island). Up to 60 people at a time, a mix of mostly college-educated Canadians and Americans, forsook a world that had created the Vietnam War and consumerism, drugs and pollution, to live in a stately stone house and tents, share their worldly goods, and seek divine guidance by going alone in the woods to perform what they called an Asking. The commune lasted less than a decade, dissolving in disarray at its last resting place amid Kingcome Inlet on the northern mainland. Lasqueti remains a sleepy, pastoral island. Its 300 or so happily isolated, mostly self-sufficient, full-time residents are served only by a foot ferry and sometime barges, and use wind, solar, and diesel power rather than BC Hydro.

If the islands themselves are fragments of the past – the peaks of sunken

Both cabin and bread are homemade at Squirrel Cove, Cortes Island.

CHRIS CHEADLE

PAUL BAILEY

64

mountains that emerged from volcanic vents in the ocean floor millions of years ago – some of their inhabitants continue to seek yesterday in them, whether it is a way of life out of the 19th century or the drop-out hippie era of the 1960s. Utopians, dreamers, urban refugees – is there a strangeness about those who settle these islands, or do the more remote islands of the Inside Passage impress their own strange auras on people?

There is always talk of ghostly presences here, routinely recorded in the literature of the coast. On Sonora Island, due east of East Thurlow, boaters have reported hearing the sound of footsteps and log-boom chains dropped on their decks at night in deserted Owen Bay – only to learn later that the bodies of two men had long ago been dragged out of the bay with boom chains binding them. Bill Wolferstan says in his sailing guide *Desolation Sound*, "an ominous feeling pervades the bay!" Liv Kennedy, a writer who grew up on these islands, records many similar stories in *Coastal Villages*. During one visit to Stuart Island, next to Sonora, she and her two older sisters slept in an abandoned house. "On several occasions during the night the rooms were flooded with light, yet there was no electricity. Locals called it the 'Haunted House.'" Gilean Douglas recounts an eerie tale in *The Protected Place*, her book about life on Cortes Island, north of Hernando and the Twins. She was living in a house owned by John Pool, who had died a decade earlier. Although she'd never met him, he had been described to her as tall, thin, and fair, which she reported in a newspaper column. One day, while looking out the window on her isolated island property, she saw a man of medium height and heft with brown hair and wearing striped overalls. When she opened the door to him, he had vanished. Soon after, an islander remarked that the description Gilean had written of Pool was all wrong. The late homeowner was really of "medium height, average build, brown hair. I remember he used to wear black-and-white striped overalls a lot."

As well as ghosts, the islands have harboured killers. In 1893, Savary's first white resident and a friend were found shot to death in his cabin; a trapper was convicted and hanged for the crime. Exactly one century later, Texada's first recorded killing occurred when a man shotgunned a fellow Torontonian transplant. Some of the badmen of the Inside Passage came from the Badlands of North Dakota. In the 1890s, half of the 60 settlers on Read Island, northwest of Cortes, were Badlanders – and among several with stained reputations was Jack Myers. During a drunken weekend on Read, fuelled by liquor he had stolen in Vancouver, he shot and killed a man in an argument over Myers's dog, Blackie, then threatened to shoot the local magistrate. It took a 17-man posse to track Myers down on the shore of an inlet; he confessed to eating Blackie in desperation a week earlier. Found

A ghost of the not-so-distant past, Denman Island.

BOB HERGER

66

guilty of manslaughter, Myers got life in prison. In the early teens of this century, Lasqueti Island was home to Henry Wagner, the Flying Dutchman, a smuggler and pirate. In a fast motorboat, with a complicated system of pipes to quiet its twin engines, he and a henchman committed armed robberies along the Pacific Northwest coast. Meanwhile, they led respectable lives on the island, even joining the Farmers' Institute. In 1913, they were trapped by the provincial police while robbing a general store on Vancouver Island; in the shoot-out, a constable died. Wagner was hanged for murder.

These islands have always had a fascinating, often bloody history. Before the Europeans arrived, the passage through them was a Native pathway – in particular, the Route of the Haida, whose marauding warriors terrorized the coast from their base in what became the Queen Charlotte Islands. Perhaps fewer than 100,000 aboriginals lived along the Pacific Northwest Coast when the white man came. They spoke six separate languages – Haida, Tlingit, Tsimishian, Kwagiulth, Nootka, and Salish – and many dialects, which marked their independence from one another. The world around them was generous, and these hunting and fishing peoples had ample time to create villages of long wooden houses heralded by totem poles signalling their social prestige. Their complex society was reflected in their art, their wood-carving, weaving, and painting, which are ranked among the greatest of primitive cultures.

The Natives of Cape Mudge make up the majority of the 2,000 people on Quadra Island which, at 276 square kilometres, is the second biggest of the Inside Passage islands. This prosperous and visually diverse island is now a 10-minute ferry ride to Campbell River on Vancouver Island, where many Quadra islanders commute to work. Quadra was originally home to the Salish, who were supplanted by the more bellicose Kwagiulth in battles at sandy, trail-lined Rebecca Spit on the island's southeastern coast. There are still signs here of a trench and embankment, part of the fortifications the Salish are believed to have built. In the 1880s, loggers were the first whites to intrude on the Kwagiulth, developing Quadra into one of the province's major timber sources; salmon fishermen, trappers, and gold and copper miners soon followed. Seafood was bountiful, and the Main Lake Chain of four linked lakes is the largest freshwater system in the southern islands (and, in this century, a lure for paddlers). Heriot Bay, above Rebecca Spit, became the supply centre for the vast Desolation Sound area, and still is for the boaters and anglers who cruise these comparatively warm waters. The historic Heriot Bay Inn has been restored to Victorian elegance; the spit is now a 175-hectare provincial marine park, rich in waterbirds. On the island's southwest shore, the family of a former publishing executive from California continues to run the April Point Lodge, heralded among the

Fishing remains a mainstay of the Inside Passage economy.

world's fly fisherfolk for its "bucktail" angling (named for the deer hair used to tie streamers to the flies) – as well as for its kitchen, which features such local delicacies as Cortes Island clams and West Coast sushi of crab and sockeye. The Cape Mudge people operate Tsa-Kwa-Luten Lodge, which features an authentic Kwagiulth feast and dance. But the most intriguing structure on the island lies immediately south, the Kwagiulth Museum and Cultural Centre. It's a treasure house of Native art repatriated from museums in eastern North America – including masks, headdresses, and copper shields seized during an illegal potlatch on nearby Village Island in 1921. The federal government, which banned potlatches between 1884 and 1951, saw the ceremonies as an excess of feasting and gift giving; to the Natives, these gatherings of clans were a way of maintaining social order, defining relationships, and redistributing wealth. Fittingly the opening of Quadra's extraordinary museum in 1979 featured a potlatch.

So did the 1992 gathering of hundreds of West Coast Natives to commemorate the investiture of a new chief and the ascension to manhood of his son at Bella Bella, north of Vancouver Island on Campbell Island. The following year, this home of the Heiltsuk Nation played host to about 1,000 members of 30 tribes who had paddled traditional cedar dugout canoes 500 kilometres and more up and down the coast, for as long as a month, to celebrate the Qatuwas festival. Bella Bella – or Waglisla, as the Heiltsuk call it – is a fishing village of 1,400 at the mouth of Dean Channel. Their houses ascend a hillside community that has revitalized itself in recent years, building new homes and apartments and developing businesses that include fishing for herring roe on kelp, a Japanese delicacy. The festival was a signpost of cultural renaissance; as internationally renowned Native artist Roy Henry Vickers said, "This is where the spirit came back to our people. It's the most important cultural event that I know of in the last 150 years."

THE COMOX TRIBE of the Coast Salish used to frequent Denman and Hornby islands, which sit side by side off Buckley Bay on Vancouver Island. Their petroglyphs and middens can still be seen here. In the 1860s and 1870s, out-of-work white loggers and miners settled this pair of islands, which are among the most livable north of the Gulfs. Eventually both were logged over, yet they keep their rural character – and, as we discovered, their islomaniac characters.

Of the two, Denman is the more suburban, a mere 10-minute ferry trip for its many middle-class commuters to Vancouver Island. A not untypical scene on Denman, a long, flat island of nearly 1,000 permanent residents on 50 square kilometres: in front of a capacious estate called Calloused Palms,

THE BENIGN KILLERS

OF THE SPECIES that live on and around these islands of the Inside Passage, none are more intriguing than the spirit bear, the six-gilled shark, and the orca – all of them man-killers of legend but not in fact.

While black bears roam some of the more northerly islands, uninhabited Princess Royal Island is among the few habitats of the remarkable white Kermode *(Ker-mode-ee)*, or snow bear. The Kermode, named for a turn-of-the-century director of what was then the B.C. Provincial Museum, is a colour variation of the so-called black bear – which can be anything from brown to blond in colour. Whether the white Kermode is a mutation or an adaptation to the Ice Age, nobody knows. It did inspire a Tsimshian legend of a spirit bear that could become human and combat evil.

Today it inspires writers and filmmakers. Sid Marty, who was a warden for 12 years in Alberta's national parks, is a poet and nature writer. For four weeks in 1993, he was on Princess Royal with documentary filmmaker Jeff Turner of Princeton, British Columbia. Biologists estimate there may be no more than 15 snow bears among 135 bears scattered through the island's 147,000 hectares of mountains, alpine meadows, and forests of spruce and cedar, fir, and hemlock. Marty found the bears here unusually trusting of the few visitors who came to the island. As he recorded one day in his journal:

On Princess Royal we observe bears in an ideal situation. They are not exposed to human garbage, so they don't connect human odour with food. They live in a calorie-rich environment of berries and salmon so they are fat and content. I would not like to generalize and call them tolerant of humans; they are tolerant of us, but we are a very atypical bunch; we all have previous experience with bears at close range.

They can be violent with each other, competing for food, but right now they don't perceive us as being threatening, or competitors. This state that they, and we, are in is as perfect as it is fragile; it is an anomaly in today's world that was probably commonplace long ago. This state of truce may be at the root of the old stories of a world where men and animals could speak to each other, and where the animals offered their power, and their flesh, to the poor, naked humans. Preserving this state of equilibrium is the most important reason for protecting this island, which could become the first black bear sanctuary in North America.

Whether or not Marty's dream is realized depends on the recommendations of a values study and socioeconomic analysis being carried out by B.C. Environment's Protected Areas Strategy. White Kermodes cannot be hunted, but black bears can – and are – by North Americans and a dozen Swiss, Austrians, and Germans who have an exclusive non-B.C.-resident hunting territory to themselves. Tsimshian Chief Neilos of Swindle Island, which lies immediately south, says Princess Royal is a sacred part of his people's tribal area. The Valhalla Society of New Denver, British Columbia, led by biologist/activist Wayne McCrory, has proposed that the two islands be designated as the Spirit Bear Wilderness Preserve, a Class A provincial marine park. Yet while these islands are contenders for preservation, there are many within B.C. Environment who consider waterfowl and seabird habitats more critical to set aside because of their high conservation values.

RICK O'NEILL

The rare Kermode bear.

If a marine park is possible to protect the white bear, perhaps there should be one for an underwater denizen, an equally rare creature off this coast: the six-gilled shark. These primitive, deep-sea sharks, with a sextet of gills and gill slits, average four metres in length and have razor-sharp teeth. A white spot on their head, some researchers believe, is a sort of translucent window linked to the six-gills' pineal gland, which senses light and might help orient the shark to the surface. On this part of the coast in summer, they cruise 20-plus metres deep along a submerged ledge of Flora Islet, off Ford's Cove at the southwest end of Hornby Island. Scuba divers swim with them and even stroke them at no apparent risk (while avoiding their hypersensitive tails). In fact, at this writing, there is no record anywhere of an unprovoked attack on humans by six-gill sharks, although they do feed on seals and large fish.

They are only one of 11 species of shark in B.C. waters, ranging from the 60-centimetre-long brown cat to the monstrous great white, the legendary, oceangoing killer shark of the *Jaws* movies. One of two great white carcasses that washed up on a Queen Charlottes beach several years ago was 5.5 metres long; a live specimen seen off the west coast of Vancouver Island was perhaps twice that length. That was one of the few great whites spotted off this coast, which is fortunate, given their many confirmed human kills in the world's warmer oceans.

There *are* marine killers threading through British Columbia's islands – orcas. But the reputation these killer whales have had until recently was somewhat undeserved. They have never been observed willfully attacking humans in the wild. There – hunting in packs and wielding their two dozen conical teeth – they are fierce and fast-thinking predators of birds, fish, turtles, squid, seals, sea lions, porpoises, and the enormous blue and grey whales. Zoologists have watched two of them tilt an ice floe with their backs and dump a seal into the awaiting mouth of a third killer whale. They also have been known to turn on one another:

in 1993, two orca-literate biologists aboard a ferry in the Inside Passage witnessed a pod of locals brawling with three transients in what they believe might have been the first recorded killer whale "rumble." But the captain of a B.C. ferry viewed another side of these so-called killers: a pair of adults kept a bloodied young orca afloat after it had been cut by the ship's propeller; two weeks later, he swears, they were still there trying to save the victim.

Orcas are members of the order *Cetacea*, which also includes dolphins, porpoises, and whales – among the 28 species of marine mammals in B.C. waters. Cetaceans are either toothed, with conical teeth to seize fish and other sizable prey, or baleen or moustached, so-called because of the flexible bonelike fibres of their enormous jaws, which filter water as they entrap much smaller sea life. Most baleen whales (such as the humpbacks, the most acrobatic of whales) have pleated throat grooves that extend as they feed.

Although nearly 400 individual orcas are known to be using Pacific Northwest waters, researchers speculate that the numbers may be significantly higher – and growing at about three percent a year. Mature males can reach 10 metres and 10 tonnes, and the triangular dorsal fin can be the height of a tall man. Orca water ballets have entertained hundreds of thousands in aquariums where their sleek bodies, with distinctive white bellies and flanks, take to the air and land with a calculated drenching of the onlookers. But they are never more gymnastic than when the male courts a female, leaping like a Barishnykov and churning the water to froth. The resulting families bond over long periods, indicating that orcas have one of the most stable societies of any mammal.

R. HAMAGUCHI

Orcas, Johnstone Strait.

only slightly more rustic than a spread in a Vancouver suburb, a home-owner sits on a mobile mower cutting an expansive lawn. But even Denman has a healthy dollop of eccentrics and artists to keep it interesting. There are the Carmen Mirandas, for instance, a trio of thirtyish women who dress up in fake-fruit hats like Hollywood's 1940s Brazilian Bombshell to entertain and inform islanders. To protest the threatened closure of the Esquimault & Nanaimo Railroad on Vancouver Island, they traipsed over to appropriately named Fanny Bay and mooned the train as it passed by. One night on Denman, they wore ferry-workers' outfits on top and fairies' costumes on bottom and did tap dances at the community hall and the ferry terminal.

And then there is an islomane like Jennie Balke, the Newt Saviour of Denman Island. A naturalist in more than heart, the slight 41-year-old with a fast and frequent laugh was trained as a large-animal veterinarian. The first cattle blood-tester in Ontario, she later worked in Zimbabwe learning how to artificially inseminate elephants. In 1988, Jennie and her partner, a resource-management consultant, bought 4.6 raw hectares on a bluff over-looking the Pacific on Denman Island.

"Why Denman?" she said when asked the obvious question. "Basically, I love the sea and the fact that you have boundaries here – so you live in a community and you know most of the people." For the first several months, Jennie and Graham lived in a tent while they began building their still-unfinished house. Since then she has leaped into island life, sitting on the animal control committee (which regulates the impact of domestic pets on wildlife) and organizing environmental seminars at the community hall, where experts speak to the locals about such subjects as forests and some of her favourite creatures – amphibians.

Jennie is quite fond of salamanders, but her particular love is the rough-skinned newt – greyish-brown on top, orange on the belly, and seldom longer than a large male hand. "Just walk along the roads at dusk near a wet area on a moist day in spring or fall," she wrote in *The Gulf Islands Guardian*, a quarterly magazine, "and you'll see dozens of motionless mini-dinosaurs trying to cross the road, often with fatal consequences. Perhaps you'll even help a few across!"

She certainly has. "Newts are such neat little animals," she told us. "They breed in the water. In winter they all go into the forest. So in some areas you get this incredible migration across the roads. When I counted 96 squished little bodies on the road in one day, I got very sad." So she built a drift fence from a tarpaulin that guided the newts into traps made from ice-cream buckets lined with moss and cotton. She then carried the creatures by hand across the highway. Among the many amphibians trapped was a long-toed salamander, the first recorded on Denman. To install the fence, she had to

PAUL BAILEY

72

get a permit from the provincial highways department. On her own, she put up signs showing a couple of newts and a message in large letters that cautioned: SLOW NEWTS XING.

And then there are those few lifelong residents of Denman, even fewer of whom are anything like cartoonist Gary Piercy. This twenty-something descendant of a prolific family that was among the first settlers has created his own whimsical universe in published comic books featuring "Funky Melow, The World of Casualism." As he explains, "It's the new religion: a laid-back, relaxed state of life. Everybody on the island seems to be very casual. If you hire somebody to do something on Tuesday, you can expect they'll be there a month later."

As a result, Denmanites do a lot for themselves. We stopped in to see Des Kennedy, who exemplifies the breed. This former Passionist monk and Children's Aid worker, 48 years old and long married to Sandy, is a story-telling eco-satirist, magazine journalist of things environmental, and gardening guru. His two bestselling books, *Living Things We Love to Hate* and *Crazy About Gardening*, are wonderfully funny while informative ("There is no vegetarian minority among spiders, no pacifist caucus; they are all killers of surpassing ingenuity and skill"). Their success has led him to national exposure as a columnist in the *Globe and Mail* and a gardening expert on CBC Television's *Midday*. A network crew comes up from Vancouver every six weeks and tapes several spots with the tall, florid-faced enthusiast with cascading red hair and bass voice. He does his stand-up monologues amid the luxuriant garden in front of the couple's third dwelling on a 4.4-hectare parcel carved out of mid-island forest (CAUTION, says the sign at the gate, SLUGS CROSSING). Spending $4,000, he and Sandy hand-built the post-and-beam house out of recycled and milled-on-the-site wood in Denman Island Eclectic style. Their first seven years here, they had no power, no running water, no phone. They lived on their vegetables and the milk and cheese of their Nubian and Alpine goats, and foraged for wild chanterelles and stinging nettles in the woods. Des picked oysters and bucked hay for a few seasons before he began writing for magazines.

Born in Liverpool and raised in Toronto, he came to the island with Sandy in 1972, seeking "someplace where we could do and be what we wanted, without undue economic pressure and the general hurly-burly that living in a city imposes on you. Which was a somewhat naive point of view because we didn't know there were nuclear warheads stored at Comox then, 16 kilometres away." Part of a wave of well-educated, long-haired young people settling in the islands, the couple were activists from the start. Through subdivision and zoning bylaws, under the aegis of the Islands

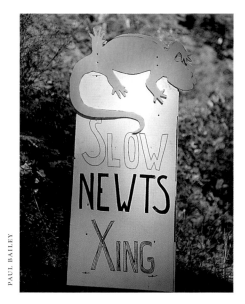

PAUL BAILEY

A road sign posted by Denman's Newt Saviour.

Opposite: On Denman, the living can be suburban – or eccentric.

Sea-carved sandstone
coastline, Hornby Island.

Trust, their generation has worked with the old-timers to help control Denman's rate and style of growth; their latest success is a land conservancy that is preserving unpopulated properties. To raise funds for the land, Sandy has been the catalyst for four annual house-and-garden tours on Denman, which one year generated $17,000. (Similar tours take place on Hornby, Saltspring, and Bowen.) The Kennedys' own terraced garden is a personal triumph, lined with local sandstone and cedar, and wedding wilderness plants with fruit trees and an English cottage-style clutter of flowering shrubs, vines, and perennials.

The next day, after a 15-minute crossing of Lambert Channel from Denman to Hornby Island, we spent the summer afternoon in another garden, this one near the tidewater of Heron Rocks. It may be less ambitious now than the Kennedys' garden, but its creator is, after all, 85 – and Hilary Brown continues to pursue her other ambitions, most of them directed at helping others. She came to Hornby in the late 1930s with her husband, Harrison Brown, who as a distinguished foreign correspondent was one of the Western world's chief witnesses to the revolution that had been wracking China. The English-born writers, visiting Vancouver Island, spotted Hornby and hired a Japanese fishing boat to take them across. Once on the 30-square-kilometre island, they roamed its plateau of fertile farmland and its fine-sand beaches and climbed up 330-metre Mount Geoffrey, until Harrison said: "I think I've seen all the beautiful views in the world but never one like this." They bought four hectares on Norman Point at the southernmost tip of the island and had a small box of a house built, grew their own vegetables, and bartered goods, while he continued to write in semiretirement. After the Second World War, they acquired 10 hectares of old-growth forest threatened with logging and, to pay the taxes, opened a campground that continues to attract many of the same families – who now own it as a cooperative.

The co-op movement fascinated Hilary, who became acting manager of Hornby's first cooperative store in 1959, then the first treasurer of its credit union, and in 1974 the first chairman of the Islands Trust that oversees Hornby and Denman as well as the Gulfs and other islands. "Because our co-op succeeded and involved people," she told us, her firm voice still hinting of England, "the immediate reaction on the island was 'we'll do it ourselves.' It's been a very healthy tendency." A decade after Harrison died in 1977, Hilary deeded her homestead to the Heron Rocks Friendship Society, which was created "to promote cross-cultural interests and look at how a rural community can contribute to the welfare of society." The experts who now come to speak at seminars and brown-bag lunches at Heron Rocks are mostly environmentalists. They are in the tradition of the internationally

BOB HERGER

known speakers who used to visit the Browns to sit beneath their enormous maple tree and discuss world issues.

The day we met her, Hilary had a floppy white hat covering her white thatch of hair, which seemed one of the few overt signs of her advancing age. She was bustling about, organizing a flood of books for a sale to raise money for an island seniors' residence, on whose board she serves. "It's my last project, I swear."

If so, it will be a surprise to Sheila McDonnell, who has run the Co-op Store for five years. "Hilary has been involved in almost every intelligent project on the island," she says. "We'd be like every other island if it wasn't for her." Among those projects was the building of a new general store a decade ago, now a $3.2-million-a-year business whose seven volunteer directors and 30 paid staff serve at least 1,700 co-op members (who pay a onetime $110 fee and can earn a three to four percent annual return from profits). The well-stocked store, with its wide verandah and surrounding shake-and-log craft shops and food outlets of the Ringside Market, is an island institution. Islanders and visitors, including transients called "shrubbies" for their outdoor sleeping habits, use it as a village centre to hang out and gossip. Another local all-in-one establishment is the recycling depot, Free Store (for reusable clothing and appliances, toys and books), and garbage transfer station. This Canadian pioneer in recycling has resulted in Hornby's producing less garbage per capita than anywhere in British Columbia by a one-to-five margin.

When the recycling depot began in 1978, the island population was about 350; it may have quadrupled since. Among the intriguing characters Hornby attracts are the architects who have fashioned unique structures of indigenous materials (Lloyd House's sod-roofed, driftwood-pillared community hall; Tim Biggin's own home of spiralled logs on stilts) and the painters, weavers, and potters who have made it known as an artists' island. High-profile Vancouverites who have places here include architect Bruno Freschi, artists Jack Shadbolt and Gordon Smith, and fine-jeweller Tony Cavelti.

Resident craftspeople are as creative in their self-sufficiency as they are in their art. For instance, potters Richard and Serena Laskin, once professors at the University of Saskatchewan, run Pizza Galore. But the most celebrated local potter/painter is Cantonese-born Wayne Ngan, whose worldwide reputation for experimental work with ceramics in a Far Eastern style no longer leaves him dependent on foraging for food and shelter. Moving to Hornby from Vancouver in 1967, Wayne and his wife at the time – Anne, a French-born artist still residing on the island – and their two daughters lived in a house that was like a piece of sculpture. Built of driftwood logs

Making it in Denman's world of funky mellow: a pair of resident potters.

PAUL BAILEY

and planks, it had station-wagon windows serving as skylights and a cylindrical steel buoy, found on the beach, filling in as a fireplace.

Wayne, who well remembers those early days when he and Anne scavenged seaweed for soups and lamb's quarter for vegetables, now lives in an elegantly simple cliffside home and studio with a serene bedroom whose moon of a window overlooks the sea. "Three days ago the ocean was gold," he told us. "You can almost eat the colour. It's like food. . . . I like the light for painting and the variety of beach – from sand to ragged to boulder to big cliff. And I like the vegetation, the trees – the nature. The island has a lot of potential for creativity, for privacy. In Vancouver so many people came every day I had to hide in the attic in my painting studio."

When we saw Wayne recently, daughter Gailan was apprenticing with him as a potter; he was back from another refuelling visit to China, where he visits family and lectures under government sponsorship. Stick-thin, sandalled, he talked gently of nature as the stuff of his art. We were in his intimate garden, flanked by willow, aspen, and 26 different types of roses, sitting beside a reposeful water-lily pond stocked with koi and carp, when he said: "See the clouds – the pond becomes a mirror of the universe. Yet suddenly a fish jumps up and splashes. It destroys everything."

That pond was once lit with floating candles and the sunset for an exquisite evening concert during the Hornby Festival of the Arts. This ambitious if underpublicized annual event is the creation of Tom Durrie, a youthful 63-year-old musician, therapist, and former teacher who directed alternative schools in Vancouver and on Saturna Island and founded Vancouver's Opera in the Schools program. In 1984, he moved to Hornby, where amateur cellist Leigh Cross had been organizing summer concerts by Canada's esteemed Purcell String Quartet. When Cross left Hornby, Durrie and other locals took over the quartet's appearances and added a jazz evening, a Noel Coward play by the island theatre group, two art films, a local artists' group show, a talk by Jack Shadbolt and, for the kids, performances by Robert Minden and his musical saw. To finance their minuscule budget, the organizers wanted to solicit funds but had no money for postage. Nora Laffin, wife of local potter Heinz Laffin, mentioned that their three-year-old son, Julian, had a bank account of family-allowance cheques. "So we asked Julian if he'd lend $200 to us," Tom recalls, "and he said, 'Yes, if you put it back.' And we did, indeed."

The budget for the Hornby Festival, which runs for 10 days in August, has grown from $2,700 to $170,000. A full-time director and an office assistant now work with a part-time but paid technical director and house manager and 50 volunteers. Performers have included contralto Maureen Forrester, tenor Richard Margison, and the 45 voices of the Canadian

Savary: early promoters called it "the South Sea Island of the North Pacific."

Children's Opera Chorus, the Danny Grossman and Jump Start dance companies, comedienne Sandra Shamas, and actor Gratien Gélinas.

The festival attracts off-islanders at a time of the year when Hornby is already at bursting point (the temporary population on a few days has reputedly reached 8,000), and some of the visitors fall victim to the island's enchantments. They hike the high bluffs and Douglas fir trails of Helliwell Provincial Park; explore the gnarled sandstone formations along Ford Cove; walk the silken sand beach at Tribune Bay (sometimes joined by nude bathers) – and, even though the island is three ferries and five hours from Vancouver, they buy.

Those who come looking for a permanent or summer place will inevitably meet Paddy Gee and her husband, Bob, who fell hard, too. She a former journalist, he a geologist, they came here from Calgary two decades ago on a visit. During a rainstorm, sitting in the living room of a funky little house on Sandpiper Beach, the only room they had seen so far, they decided to buy the property and change their lives. They also bought an Ontario 32 sailboat, appropriately named *Gone Bananas*, and skippered it on charter cruises to help support themselves. Then the island's real-estate agent, retiring to paint, convinced Paddy to take her place. In 1989, she was Realty World's International Rookie of the Year for residential sales. Bob has since joined her selling houses; they now own a handsome, contemporary 297-square-metre home with an indoor pool and, as the Gees might say, a spectacular ocean view. Their boat? It's moored in Comox, where they occasionally get to sleep on it.

The pace of real-estate sales on Hornby has meant the price of a very basic house on an inland one-fifth hectare has doubled to $150,000 in two years, and that has put more pressure on island resources. Yet residents remain adamant about trying to preserve the way of life they came here for. They are pleased to have a seasonal RCMP officer and year-round auxiliary patrolman to control the invasions of vacationing young people who in recent years have made the island a Fort Lauderdale Northwest. And despite the inconvenience – or rather because of it – islanders continue to demand that the ferry service shut down each night at 6:00 p.m.

IN 1978, THE SAME YEAR the Gees moved to Hornby, Californian Juanita Chase and her Canadian husband came to Savary Island to transform their lives. They bought a hotel that closed after two seasons, and like Paddy Gee, Juanita found herself selling real estate – among other things. She has handled cottage rentals, run the island propane-supply business, driven the land taxi, been custodian of the water district and secretary-treasurer of the volunteer fire department, and cofounded the *Savary Island News*. As the

Petroglyphs on Berry Island, in the Broughton Archipelago east of Malcolm Island.

CHRIS CHEADLE

population increases, with her help, she says, "I feel there's a need for structure on the island, but I'm terrified of what the structure will be."

On bikes borrowed from Juanita, we cycled to the Front – or Front Row, Wharf End, and Malaspina Boulevard – where a flotilla of about 60 dwellings, many of them gracious old homes, face Keefer Bay. We visited with octogenarian Lorencia Rickard, the fourth generation of her family to live on the island. She and husband Hugh still spend several months of the year in a Pan-Abode powered in part by solar energy. Most of the properties on the Front have never changed hands, and the Rickards would like to keep it that way. "It was a lovely, peaceful island, and it still is, except in summer," she told us. Down the road is the family property of Daryl Duke, the well-travelled Canadian film and TV director (*The Thorn Birds, Tai-pan*). "If there's any place I think of home, it's here," he told us. His wife, Ann-Marie, said Savary is "where he finds his peace, his inner self, his soul." Mid-island, definitely not on the Front, we found Bill Palfrey, the other resident realtor, who a decade earlier had moved his business here from Victoria at age 64. The place he built looking out to Desolation Sound has a cowbelled gate bearing the sign UNSAVARY MANOR. Bill wears cutoff jeans, a beard, and a bluebird tattoo. "I enjoy beachcombing," he said, "and watching the eagles and trying to keep the deer out of my garden. And now I have peacocks to brighten things up." He had eight peacocks at the time we visited, and chickens, a dog, and a paddock for the horses he hoped to bring in, an experiment with two donkeys having failed. "If you're going to be a squire, you need the trappings."

That evening we had dinner with friends on the deck of their home-made cabin at Indian Point. We began with beheaded prawns, plump and pink in their shells, fresh that day from local waters. The day before, Sheila had dug littleneck clams on the beach, just two minutes down the forest path, and put them through several rinses to clean them of sand. We had them with garlic butter, slightly burnt but the better for it. The main course was surf-and-turf, Savary style: a salmon that a neighbour had caught only that morning, grilled teriyaki-style on the barbecue, along with a meltingly tender filet mignon from a mainland butcher who delivers to the island. Then we took the motorboat out with our friends' granddaughter and putted into the sunset, recalling the description of Savary by one of Captain George Vancouver's crew when they happened upon the island on a July evening two centuries ago: ". . . a delightfull plain with a fine smooth beach before it for the Boats, that renderd the situation both desirable & pleasant & such as they of late seldom enjoyd."

An escarpment rises steeply from the Denman shore.

PAUL BAILEY

GUNTER MARX

SCENES FROM A LONELY LAND

THE AUGUST MOON above the North Pacific beach was full – bright and high. Washed by its light, Jim Hart was telling us the story of how humankind was born right here. Here on this sandy spit at the northeastern verge of the islands that the original inhabitants continue to call Haida Gwaii, more than two centuries after an English explorer named them for his ship, the *Queen Charlotte*. Hart is a Haida carver, 41 when we met, with a ponytail of coal-black hair and a wispy beard and moustache. He is steeped in the old stories of his people, one of which he was relating with his own twist: "The Raven is kind of hungry all the time. He's walking along the edge of this beach and all of a sudden sees this clamshell on the bottom of the ocean and these little critters be-bopping around the edge of the shell. He sees them and dives down into the ocean and grabs them and pulls them out. They look like men and women things. They're just people, right? Playing together. He hauls them up on the beach – and then the fun starts."

Story told, we were strolling off Rose Spit in Naikoon Provincial Park when headlights approached us on the beach. Two dune buggies rumbled across the sand. Humankind was still be-bopping around. It was a reminder that civilization has had its way with these islands, the most isolated off either end of Canada, but that – like the tide that will wash away the buggies' tracks – the Queen Charlottes have managed so far to contain the excesses, keeping the little critters in their place.

MINING, LOGGING, and now tourism have all shored up the economy of the 150 or so lonely, lovely islands and endless islets that form a fat exclamation point at the edge of the continent. Nearer Alaska than to the rest of Canada, this 250-kilometre-long archipelago (about a third the area of Vancouver Island) is separated from the islands of mainland British Columbia by an average of 100 kilometres of the open sea of Hecate Strait.

The evergreen Graham Island, Queen Charlottes.

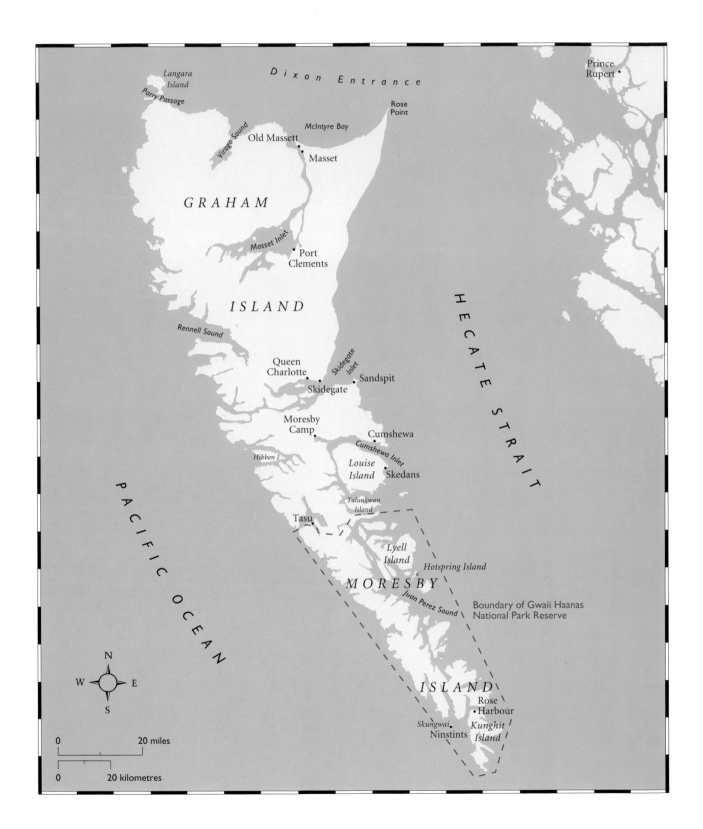

Dixon Entrance

Langara Island

Parry Passage

Virago Sound

McIntyre Bay

Rose Point

Prince Rupert •

Old Massett •

Masset •

GRAHAM

Masset Inlet

Port Clements •

ISLAND

Rennell Sound

HECATE STRAIT

Queen Charlotte •

Skidegate Inlet

Skidegate •

Sandspit •

Moresby Camp •

Cumshewa •

Cumshewa Inlet

Hibben I

Louise Island

Skedans •

Talunkwan Island

Tasu •

PACIFIC OCEAN

Lyell Island

Hotspring Island

MORESBY

Juan Perez Sound

Boundary of Gwaii Haanas National Park Reserve

N
W   E
S

ISLAND

Rose Harbour •

Skungwai
Ninstints

Kunghit Island

0   20 miles

0   20 kilometres

Its seclusion hasn't prevented people from appreciating the sumptuousness of its wildlife and rare plants, its melange of microclimates, its mountainous land and misted waterscapes – and from exploiting the richness of its gold mines and rainforests. Yet one of the nation's seminal environmental battles was won here when the federal government agreed in 1987 to set aside one-third of the islands as the Gwaii Haanas National Park Reserve and Haida Heritage Site. Today it is co-managed by Parks Canada and the powerful Native people who call themselves the Haida Nation.

We hadn't been to the Queen Charlottes since 1974. Returning two decades later, we knew the population had risen to about 5,400 from 4,250. The islands no longer felt quite as secluded, were no longer linked only by radio-telephone to the the rest of the world. Air service had doubled to two flights a day, and in 1980 a 90-vehicle BC Ferries vessel began making several runs a week from Prince Rupert on the mainland. We passed up the seven-hour ferry trip for a Fokker F-28 jet that took just 75 minutes to fly 650 kilometres from Vancouver. A Haida mother sat across the aisle reading storybooks to her daughter; six middle-aged men behind us were anticipating a fishing trip in the Charlottes, saying things like: "We're not going to bother with halibut. We're going after whales."

The superb saltwater fishing for mighty halibut and salmon attracts commercial fleets as well as the world's more adventurous anglers. Lakes and streams run fat with salmon and steelhead (former American President Jimmy Carter devoted a chapter in *An Outdoor Journal* to Moresby steelhead fishing, which he considered among the finest on the continent). Hunters come for the abundant small deer and the biggest of all black bears. Nature lovers come to watch the grey whales (and 10 other cetaceans) during their migration between Mexico and Alaska; the innumerable bald eagles, the thickest nesting of peregrine falcons in the country, and the breeding grounds for a quarter of all the seabirds on our Pacific coast; and unique subspecies of marten and hairy woodpeckers. Then there is the flora, such as an alpine lily variation and the yellow perennial daisy *Senecio newcombei*, seen only here. Pockets of these islands missed the glaciation that shrouded the rest of British Columbia. This, together with their isolation, helps explain why the flora and fauna are so different from those of the mainland. The tectonic forces that shaped the Charlottes continue to make them the most earthquake-prone region in Canada (in 1949, the country's worst quake, measuring 8.1 on the Richter scale, shook the west coast of the islands).

We landed at the evocatively named settlement of Sandspit on the northernmost tip of Moresby Island, just south of the other major island, Graham. Here on the islands' eastern shores there isn't any more precipitation than in Vancouver, but the western flanks can endure triple the rainfall

BOB HERGER

and be whipped by winds that might reach 200 kilometres per hour. This evening the moist air wasn't far off the average August temperature of 17 degrees Celsius. A lone bald eagle awaited in the intermittent rain. Touching down, we whispered to one another, "It's magical."

The 550 people who live along the grassy flats of Sandspit have traditionally depended on the airport and on the logging of the grandest conifers in Canada. Since the creation of the park reserve in 1987, no logging has been allowed there and residents have seen their incomes drop steeply. As compensation under the terms of the park agreement, locals were hoping for a major harbour that would attract more tourists, including cruise-ship passengers. But it was not until the late summer of 1994 that the federal government announced a new $38 million development fund for the islands and a further $10 million to build and operate harbour facilities. In our first encounter with a debate between loggers and environmentalists that splits the islands like the sea, our landlady for the night urged us to talk to all kinds of people here – not just the Haida. "*They* call it Haida Gwaii [Islands of the People]. But it's not. It's the Queen Charlottes. It belongs to all of us."

What draws many visitors, however, is the living legacy of the artistic and artful Haida people, who have been here anywhere from 6,000 to 10,000 years, and whose long-abandoned villages with their toppled totem poles are among the world's historical treasures. About a third of the population, they exert an influence that pervades the life of the islands. It is most visible in and around Skidegate, a Native community of 500 on Graham Island, a brief ferry ride across Skidegate Inlet from Sandspit. Here in the Queen Charlotte Islands Museum, a longhouse-like structure of cedar and glass above the inlet, the history and art of the Haida are accessibly displayed. Among its treasures are totems and mortuary poles commemorating high-ranking dead, intricate baskets, and remarkable bent-wood boxes that are steamed and bent in three places to form a watertight container from a single plank. Some of the artifacts are repatriated, including a Raven headdress taken from Skidegate in 1883 and exhibited until recently at the Smithsonian Institution in Washington, D.C.

A modern totem of unstained cedar rises beside the longhouse of the Skidegate Band Council office, down the road from a community health centre and Dave's Fast Food concession. Designed by Bill Reid, a master carver and metalsmith of mixed Haida and white descent, the 18-metre-high Dogfish Pole was the first in nearly a century to be raised at Skidegate. We watched a bald eagle perched atop the dogfish fin, his golf ball of a head turning from time to time to scan the water and the grassy field below. The Charlottes – Haida Gwaii – were working their magic.

Wildflowers, Hotspring Island, Queen Charlottes.

THE NEXT MORNING we asked Jeff King, publisher of the *Queen Charlotte Islands Observer*: "Who runs this place?" Lean, shod in sandals, and sporting a salt-and-pepper beard, King sat at his desk, which was topped with an Apple computer, and pondered the question. "Who runs this place? The Haida run a large part of it. Lots of things don't happen unless the Haida agree to it. They believe every last square inch of the Queen Charlottes belongs to them. They *do* exclude privately held land – and we *are* welcome guests of the Haida."

He admires them for their single-mindedness: "The Haida are as clever players as you'll come across. They're fully focused on the long term to an extent that surprises me. They want the land claims settled in their favour, and everything they do advances that cause. They've been consistent and they've been doing well. A few years ago a lot of them destroyed their [Canadian] passports and got their own and had various countries stamp them. They don't miss a trick."

King, his wife, Diane, and their two teenage children live in a contemporary cedar house overlooking the sea on Graham Island, just west of Skidegate. Their weekly newspaper office, bookstore, and a printing business run by Diane are a five-minute drive away in the unincorporated community of Queen Charlotte, an administrative centre of 1,000 residents. The first townsite on the islands, this regional district is a century old and is a sometimes-charming bowling alley of a place strung out along the waterfront. The Kings have been here for a decade; they decided to buy the idiosyncratic local newspaper after being bewitched on a family camping trip by the Charlottes' grandeur and an unseasonable sunny spell. "As a Winnipegger," King said, "my whole life is based on getting away from cold weather."

Once they moved here the honeymoon was brief. "People see the islands as a paradise of relaxation," he said, "but I never worked so hard in my life. I've been on my sailboat once all summer. You have to be more self-reliant here. When storms start howling through and the ferry is stuck in Rupert and groceries are running low, you think of yourself on the edge of the unknown universe. It's almost impossible to get a plumber when the water in your house stops running, so you learn to do your own plumbing. You can buy just about anything on the islands you need" – Charlotte, as locals call it, has a video shop and a health-food store, for instance – "but you'll probably pay more and you won't have a choice. Rupert hotels are full of islanders shopping at Christmastime." Other complications arise. "I've heard that 40 percent of the islanders are new every five years; I've gone

Dogfish Pole, Council Band Office, Skidegate.

92

through all kinds of good friends." In his newspaper, King prefers to run a range of passionately expressed letters to the editor rather than write his own editorials. "People have firmly held convictions on virtually every subject, and there is a tension between Charlotte and Masset – every community is very protective of its own turf."

The next day we drove 100 kilometres up-island to the fishing and military town of Masset. The first third of the good two-lane highway parallels the Pacific. Soon we were pulling over at a rest stop, guarded by wood carvings of a bear and an eagle, to walk the long curve of a wide beach of welcoming sand instead of the usual boulders. Dragonflies helicoptered around us; the pleasant pungency of seaweed spiked the warm air. We'd pause again near Tlell, where the road turns inland. For a settlement the length of a wink, it had several artisans' studios, a lingering reflection of the hundreds of counter-culture settlers who escaped to the Charlottes during the early 1970s. In her Crystal Cabin, Laura Dutheil was making collector's-quality dolls of fibre, stone, precious metals, and feathers – what she called spirit dolls. "Spirituality here is more in tune with nature – not like a religion, more like a goodwill message – and I encourage people to use the dolls as a tool of strength, of comfort and of healing."

On the road north, nature was at her most pastoral, most healing. We met two backpackers on bicycles; with only a couple of hills, the highway is a cyclist's dream. At about the same time, amid open range that had been homesteaded after the turn of the century, we saw our first cattle and horses. Humans want to make their mark in a more indelible manner south of the forest-based town of Port Clements (population: 500), where several companies have tried to develop a gold mine. But the Haida Nation, among others, has opposed the project as a potential threat to the nearby Yakoun River, a prolific sockeye salmon stream where the Haida have been coming to fish for food for decades, if not centuries.

Hungry for the wilder landscape we remembered, we drove down a gravel logging road near Port Clements, in search of one of a half-dozen or more golden spruce discovered on the islands. Because these genetic malformations have too little of a pigment protecting them from excessive light, photo-oxidation partially breaks down the chlorophyll that should turn their needles green. We walked for five minutes along the lyrical Yakoun River, down a rainforest trail that took us through great green spruce, their lower limbs whiskered with moss. There, on the opposite bank, a little like an evergreen gilded for Christmas, was a three-century-old, 50-metre-tall golden spruce.

Looming on the horizon near Masset was a man-made phenomenon, a Canadian Forces spy station. The skyscraping circular radar fence that

Dolomite (or Burnaby) Narrows between South Moresby and Burnaby islands.

enclosed the surveillance facility reminds one Haida resident of "an elephant pen." At 33, its commanding officer, Major Scott McLean, was only ten years older than the station. He described its work (carefully) as the "collection of signals intelligence, geo-location in support of the Canadian cryptologic program, and high-frequency direction-finding in support of search-and-rescue missions."

"Can we presume which countries we're listening to?" we asked him.

"You can, but I can't. But if you look at our location, you can guess. . . . Speaking personally, I believe the world is a less stable place than it has been in the last 40 years. As witness what's going on in Bosnia-Herzegovina, the Pacific Rim heating up, and – regardless of the Soviet Union disintegrating – they still have all those weapons."

Not long after we visited, CFS Masset faced drastic cuts as the federal government downsized or eliminated military bases across Canada. It had been employing about 80 civilians as well as 260 military members who lived with their 380 dependents in housing units that looked as if they were airlifted from a Toronto suburb. The station had its own store, two schools, three messes, a 13-bed hospital, a nine-hole golf course, a curling rink, and the best-equipped recreation centre on the islands (swimming pool, squash court, sports field) – all of which, except for the schools, had been open to the people of Masset and the nearby Native village of Old Massett. Although the members of the military received an isolation allowance, which meant they lived virtually rent-free, the outdoor lifestyle and sense of community seemed to make up for any sense of seclusion. Major McLean said that, during a recent tour by the Canadian Forces' chief of Defence Staff, "only one person told him he was counting the days till he would leave."

When the defence chief visited, the wives of the VIPs were entertained at a dinner catered by David Phillips, who runs Copper Beach House, the lovingly, eccentrically adorned bed-and-breakfast where we stayed in Masset. He's a grey-bearded Buddha of a man who in 1991, from the wilds of Masset, organized the launch of an exhibition called "The Spirit of Haida Gwaii" at the Canadian Embassy in Washington, D.C. It was the biggest and most sophisticated work of his friend, the artist Bill Reid: a five-tonne canoe cast in bronze and bearing 13 carved figures from Native mythology. Phillips arranged for 50 representatives of the Haida Nation to attend the opening and stage a potlatch, an ancient ceremony in which Natives once gave away much of their wealth to show their status in an extended clan and to repay relatives who had helped them in some way.

Bill Reid has described the figures in the canoe as "symbols of another time when the Haidas, all ten thousand of them, knew they were the greatest

NINSTINTS

One autumn evening a decade ago, cinematographer Karl Spreitz and a colleague were resting against a log on a little bay at Ninstints, on Skungwai, the most southerly and remote of the Queen Charlotte Islands. As the sun set on the other side of the deserted island, a strange, lovely light blurred the eastern shore and the sea before them. Nearby was the sheltered crescent of a beach where the world's finest existing stand of totem poles rises on its original site. The poles, tilting toward one another, and the fallen, rotting posts and beams of 17 houses were evocative vestiges of the once-awesome Haida culture that had terrorized the West Coast with its might and skill. The presence of these remnants was so impressive that a year earlier, in 1984, UNESCO had declared this a World Heritage Site, "of importance to the history of Mankind."

By now, filming a documentary about Ninstints, Karl had no doubt that there was an alien air to this village abandoned around 1880. So he watched in silence and some wonderment as three small craft unexpectedly appeared offshore. Their occupants emerged and began moving through what seemed like deep water, but coming closer their silhouettes still appeared to be half the size of humans.

It was only when they reached the shore and began fitting on their prosthetic legs that he realized they were amputees who had kayaked three wave-lashed kilometres off the western tip of Houston Stewart Channel to partake of the myth and legend of Skungwai.

Few people have seen the island once called Anthony, but that now goes by its Haida name (which means Red Cod Island). It was here, on 138 hectares in the shape of a bird in flight, that hundreds of Kunghit warriors lived along the shore in longhouses crafted from the same cedar they used to carve the poles that stood inside and in front of their homes. Cedar so soft and light, yet so strong, so straight of grain and free of knots, that it could be hewn into 12-metre planks, 10 centimetres thick, and so rich with different oils that it is among the most durable of woods. Such trees were the building blocks of a rich world created by these hunters of the sea on the edge of a continent.

That world began to shatter in 1787 when they met and traded sea otter pelts with the British Captain George Dixon and his crew of the *Queen Charlotte*. News of the valuable furs attracted other traders, including the American John Kendrick who, angered by the Kunghits' petty thefts, seized two chiefs and threatened them with death. The capture was particularly humiliating for Chief Hoyeh (Haida for "Raven," the name of the island's major lineage), who three days later made a return visit to Kendrick's ship with 150 of his people. When a third

of them were allowed on board, they began ransacking the *Lady Washington.* Her crew wielded guns and cutlasses to kill 40 of the men, women, and children. Hoyeh's later attacks on two other ships were a bloody success, but in 1795 he and perhaps 70 Kunghit died ignominiously in their assault on the 17-man sloop *Union.*

A successor – Chief Ninstints of the Eagle lineage, He-Who-Is-Equal-to-Two – would prove to be more revered, having given 10 potlatches that might well have inspired some of the totem poles that still stand on the site that bears his name. The wealth the sea otter trade brought the Kunghit and other Haida gave rise to their first professional class of artists.

But the white man's presence also brought pestilence. Around 1840, there were 308 Haida living at Ninstints; 40 years later, there were 30. Most of the dead were victims of smallpox, in an epidemic that swept up the Pacific Northwest Coast after an infected passenger landed in Victoria on a ship from San Francisco in 1862. The few surviving Kunghit eventually assimilated into the Haida tribe at Skidegate.

In 1957, contemporary Haida artist Bill Reid and a museum work party came by ship to the forsaken village. In a salvage expedition sponsored by Vancouver lumber baron and Native art collector Walter C. Koerner, they cut down and removed 11 of the best-preserved totem poles –

some 16 metres tall, weighing several tonnes – and brought them to the Museum of Anthropology in Vancouver and the Royal British Columbia Museum in Victoria. Most were mortuary or grave poles, at the top of which chiefs had been buried in boxes bearing their crests. Now bleached of their earth-pigment hues of black and red, the sculptures still show the details that distinguish Haida carving: intertwined figures, humans with ravens and whales; protruding tongues; and all-seeing eyes sculpted in a stylized oval shape called ovoid, with tension at their corners and pupils slightly bulging.

Today, amid fragments of longhouses, 26 poles remain, many of them toppled. Crews have cleaned them of moss and foliage and cleared surrounding trees and brush. The poles and the island affect visitors in varying ways. One writer who stayed in Ninstints overnight many years ago woke up screaming. Photographer Russ Heinl, who spent a day here recently, felt surrounded by people who were no longer present, "as if children were still playing in the water and we couldn't see them. It wasn't a bad feeling." Filmmaker Spreitz says simply, "It was the most incredible cathedral I've ever been in."

Although the surviving poles are wondrous, they are only plaintive symbols of what has been lost here. These monuments of master carvers, Reid writes in *Out of the Silence,* "were objects of bright pride, to be admired in the newness of their crisp curved lines, the powerful flow of sure elegant curves and recesses – yes, and in the brightness of fresh paint. They told the people of the completeness of their culture, the continuing lineages of the great families, their closeness to the magic world of myth and legend."

GUNTER MARX

of all nations." When Spanish sea captain Juan Pérez first sighted the islands in 1774, they may have been home to more than 7,000 Haida; others lived to the north, in what became the Alaskan Panhandle. Like their language, which is unrelated to any other, they remain singular among Northwest Coast Native people. The Inside Passage, from what is now Puget Sound in Washington State to Skagway in southeastern Alaska, was once the route of the Haida, who raided villages and traded slaves along its 1,600-kilometre length. Haida warriors were imposing figures, fierce in their painted faces and tattooed skins, some of them standing much taller than most aboriginal and European people of the time. Their cedar dugout canoes were technological as well as artistic triumphs: up to 23 metres long, they could carry 40 men and more than two tonnes of freight. The abundance of sea life allowed the Haida to develop a complex society symbolized by the sophisticated designs of totem poles and other carvings of cedar, precious metals, and argillite, a local black slate. In the 19th century, after they began trading prized sea otter pelts with the Europeans and Americans, the Haida paid a horrific price: within two years in the 1860s, the white man's smallpox had reduced their numbers on the islands by 70 percent. At the turn of the century, the survivors abandoned their southern villages to settle on Graham Island.

Resonances of their encounters with non-Natives continue. There are suicides, some drug and alcohol abuse, and even an arson fire of a church and longhouse in Masset several years ago. Yet we realized that these people remain among the proudest of all Native groups in North America, never signing a single treaty with any government. One sign of their self-confidence is the Haida Gwaii Rediscovery Camp, which helps strengthen the presence of Haida culture among the young people of the islands. The Haida camp sparked a larger Rediscovery movement that numbers 15 camps, primarily for Native youth, in Canada, the United States, and New Zealand. It was launched in 1978 by an American draft resister living on the islands, Thom Henley, and a local Native carver, dancer, and singer. Gary Edenshaw, the stocky, bearded artist, now calls himself by a Haida name, Guujaaw (pronounced *Gooj-ow*), and we were to meet him a few days later down south. First we sought out his son, Gwaii (*Gwy*), who lives with his white mother in Masset, next door to David Phillips.

Gwaii's name means "island" in Haida – "just so they can't say, 'No man is an island,'" Guujaaw would tell us with a smile. The 17-year-old Gwaii, blue-eyed, pale-complected, had much of his poet mother in him. But he reflected his father in a fierce loyalty to his Haida heritage: the following year, Gwaii was in Vancouver as an apprentice artist under the tuition of Bill Reid and, since 1988, has been involved each summer as a participant and

junior guide at the Rediscovery Camp on the northwest coast of Graham Island. This wilderness camp on Taalung Slung Bay draws on the strengths of Native tradition "to help youth discover and respect the world within themselves, the cultural worlds between them, and the world around them." Guujaaw pointed out that "there are a lot of kids' camps around that are based on conquering the land – you go out and beat that mountain – but at Rediscovery Camp they learn how they fit into the natural world." It's supported by the elders of the community, who have often taught there.

The previous summer, 10 teens in one session and 13 pre-teens in another, non-Native boys and girls included, lived in longhouses on the sandy beach; foraged the sea for such food as devilfish and octopus; hiked for six days along the craggy west coast; played nature-appreciation games in the forest and on the shore; visited abandoned village sites to learn Haida history; and each did a 24-hour solo retreat armed with only three matches, a potato, water, and a sleeping bag. Gwaii told us he has made many of his best friends at Rediscovery, perhaps himself among them. Recalling his solo experience at age 11, he said "that's where I and a lot of people get strength of character. You're forced to be with yourself and I was afraid of the dark – and coping with that was a major difficulty. I felt I got closer to nature." The youngest participant in the 1993 camp, a 10-year-old white boy named Martin Hermanek, said: "If you can do the solo, you can do anything. I felt joy because I did it. I want to go there next year."

Martin lives in Masset, where his parents run a restaurant. The largest community on the islands, with a population of 1,500, it is also the closest in character to a conventional small town. Run by a mayor and council, it has a recognizable residential section, four churches, a playground and a tennis court, a car lot called Isolated Auto Sales, even a neighbourhood pub known as Daddy Cool's.

The nearby Delkatla Wildlife Sanctuary is a crucial link on the Pacific Flyway, harbouring 132 species of birds, including the densest nesting of Least sandpipers in the world, on nearly 200 hectares of mudflat, marsh, and meadow land. Just northwest of here, 700 Haida live in the original village of Masset, built on three ancient Native village sites facing Masset Sound. Old Massett – its newest name – is graced with several contemporary totem poles.

We found Jim Hart there, chopping and chiselling another totem pole for an American private collector. "I'm carving my way to heaven," he said. His great-grandfather on his mother's side was Charles Edenshaw, one of the greatest of all Haida sculptors; his father is a white man from Ontario who worked at the military base in Masset. The son is another student of Bill Reid, who assisted the master carver at the University of British Columbia's

Haida button blanket, Skidegate.

99

BOB HERGER

Museum of Anthropology to create the monumental cedar sculpture, *Raven and the First Men.* The old story commemorated in this 1980 work was one Hart would tell us on the beach at Rose Spit. "The stories you learn are not just myth," he said later as we drove south to Old Massett on a gravel road through a night as black as argillite. "When you get into a jam, a story pops into your mind and it takes you right through it." Now he needed the help of those tales he learned from his great-aunts. His career splits his time between Vancouver, where he flies every few weeks to do business, and the islands, where he has his roots. "I find at home here we're still who we are. We haven't been tromped on by outside influences. . . . When you come from the islands, there's an attitude – there's nothing better."

But we still hadn't seen the best of the islands. The next day we boarded a rigid-frame Polaris inflatable boat, roomy enough for 11 passengers and a guide named Ian Gould, and headed down the coast to the Gwaii Haanas National Park Reserve. The Haida name means "a place of wonder" – a superlative we would soon embrace.

A black bear fishes Echo Harbour in Darwin Sound, Gwaii Haanas.

Ian's brother, Doug, runs Moresby Explorers, one of several tour companies plying the southern inlets in summer. Both men are locally born loggers. Uncertain of their futures on the Charlottes since the 90-kilometre-long archipelago became a park reserve, they now hope to make some of their living from selectively showing off a wildland whose cedar and pine, hemlock and spruce are forever off-limits to any commercial chain saw. The area was saved after the Haida Nation made a stand on Lyell Island, off the northwestern coast of South Moresby. The original impetus for the action had come long before, from Thom Henley and Guujaaw, the same pair who would later create the Rediscovery camps to preserve Haida history and culture. In 1974, alarmed at clearcut logging on the Charlottes, they started the Islands Protection Committee, drawing a line across South Moresby that enclosed Lyell Island. The following year the B.C. government granted a forest company a licence to cut Lyell's virgin stand of old-growth timber. For the next decade, it would clearcut there. The Haida-backed protection committee kept protesting, while a Sandspit-based group called Moresby Island Concerned Citizens would support the logging. At one point its leader was Doug Gould's father, Duane, the owner of a local garage and more recently Sandspit's regional director.

Although federal officials talked of resolving Haida land issues in South Moresby and creating a park, the provincial government allowed logging to continue. On an October day in 1985, 30 Haida men and women, Guujaaw among them, successfully blockaded the road to the logging camp on Lyell.

"We considered everything from armed insurrection to passive resistance," he recalled. In the ensuing weeks, female elders in traditional button blankets and young Haida men in battle paint blocked the logging trucks, the RCMP arrested them (one Native Mountie cried as he led away his 67-year-old aunt, Ethel Jones), and lawyers for both sides fought the legal fight in court. The resulting furor attracted international media attention, moral support from key U.S. conservation groups, and financial support from singers Pete Seeger and Bruce Cockburn. In 1986, the B.C. government announced a moratorium on further logging in South Moresby. A year later, the federal government agreed to preserve the entire area from Lyell Island southward. And in 1990, Ottawa signed an agreement with the Haida Nation to share planning, operation, and management of the area. It is an innovative agreement in which the Haida claim the southern archipelago as their hereditary lands and the government says it will co-manage Gwaii Haanas as a park reserve pending the resolution of any legal Haida land claim. As Bill Reid wrote, "These shining islands may be the signposts that point the way to a renewed harmonious relationship with this, the only world we're ever going to have."

Haida Watchmen act as caretakers at key abandoned Native villages in the National Park Reserve and Haida Heritage Site.

BOB HERGER

OF FISH AND FISHERS

BENEATH THE SEA and in the sky above Haida Gwaii are the ocean and avian life that attracts so many visitors to these islands – most prominently, salmon and their predators, bald eagles.

British Columbia has five species of salmon: pink, chum, coho, sockeye, and that most-prized game fish, the chinook. Pinks are the smallest, generally weighing about 2.2 kilograms; chinook are the largest, ranging up to 30 kilograms (average-sized chinook are called springs; those over 13.5-kilograms are called tyees). Recent conservation measures for the endangered chinook have been encouraging, and the Queen Charlottes still offer some of the biggest, usually caught by slowly trolling a cut-plug herring bait. The islands' luxurious, isolated lodges lure wealthy, publicity-shy guests, such as Malaysian Robert Kuok, 14th in *Forbes* magazine's ranking of world billionaires, who after landing a 15.4-kilogram salmon off the Charlottes in 1988, decided British Columbia was so wonderful that he stopped off in Vancouver and bought $80 million worth of development property.

In the water and beneath the sand lie other creatures: a feast of edible clams, oysters, shrimp, prawns, Dungeness and red rock crabs, mussels, sea urchins, cockles, and scallops (abalone harvesting has been prohibited in recent years as a conservation measure). Clam varieties include native littlenecks and accidentally introduced Japanese littlenecks; delicious razors; abundant butters; and large and grotesque-looking geoducks (pronounced *gooee-ducks*) – all of which are dug out of the sand with garden rakes, potato forks, and shovels. Just offshore and in tide pools lurks colourful, imaginatively christened marine life: bat ray sea stars, moon snails, sea cucumbers, goose barnacles, brooding anemones, and cryptic nudibranchs (nearly transparent members of a group less genteelly known as sea slugs). And deep down are octopi, including the giant Pacific species, which can weigh 45 kilograms and have an armspread of six metres; and flying squid, a favourite of Japanese fishing fleets, which have harvested them with walls of drift nets extending for 45 kilometres or more.

Among the finest fishers of all – especially of salmon – are bald eagles, which are so pervasive on the Charlottes. More live on the Pacific Northwest Coast than anywhere else in the world, and British Columbia alone has as many as 15,000 adults – a population that can double when juveniles join them in flocks of up to a thousand for the winter salmon runs. The eagles bond for keeps, generally occupying a single nest (which can weigh a tonne) throughout their average 38-year lifetime. Although they are still considered endangered in the United States, their population along this shoreline is stable. Adult balds, with their white heads and tails and yellow talons and beaks, stand up to a metre tall

CHRIS CHEADLE

and have wingspans as wide as 2.4 metres. They can fly 48 kilometres per hour, plunge at 160, and detect a trout 1.5 kilometres away. They will eat small mammals and birds, abalone and other shellfish, but as scavengers they prefer carrion and even garbage.

The prince of scavengers in the bird world might well be the raven. This trickster of Native mythology, endowed with mystical powers, gave its name to one of the Haida's two traditional extended clans (the other was named for the eagle). Sixty centimetres or more in length, with a wingspan double that in width, and a weight about quadruple the American crow's, the glistening black raven also differs from its relative in other ways. It has pointed rather than blunt wings, a long wedge of a tail in place of a square one, and a mostly caw-less vocabulary that may be second only to humans'. Ravens sing musically in choirs and coo softly and tenderly to their mates-for-life. In scavenging and hunting, they demonstrate their remarkable intelligence – for instance, working in teams to kill newborn reindeer fawns, with some of them separating the mother from the infant, which the others then savage.

Of the 16 million seabirds in the province – including gulls and terns, cormorants and mergansers – the most plentiful of all are the murres and murrelets, auklets and puffins of the Alcids species, which inhabit remoter reaches of the coast. On Reef and Limestone islands in the Charlottes, near the abandoned Native village of Skedans, ancient murrelets nest under tree roots in the old-growth forests. Canadian Wildlife Service (CWS) researchers there have unearthed some fascinating facts about the murrelets: in the first two days of parenting in burrows, adults and their chicks imprint one another's calls so that when the babies then paddle perhaps a dozen kilometres out to sea while their parents fly out, they can reunite by sound alone. The Laskeek Bay Conservation Society, under CWS supervision, is banding the birds on Limestone Island, using plastic sheeting to funnel the chicks to six narrow openings. In summer, the society will show kayakers and tour-boat visitors around the island to observe the murrelets. Christine Atkins, a graduate student in biology, says, "On a good night hundreds of prospectors – unmated birds – can be 40 metres up in the trees, or on the ground, and actually sing to attract females with a complex bubbling, popping, *electric* sound."

CHRIS CHEADLE

Cormorants are prominent among British Columbia's 16 million seabirds.

Doug Gould remained disappointed that the government didn't exempt Lyell and two other islands from the agreement. "I was born here," he said. "This is my land, too. Ninety-five percent of the Charlottes has been public land. The Haida have been running it all these years. But they have to share it." For the past six seasons he and his brother had been sharing this land they love, taking visitors out in a Polaris, smaller Zodiacs, and kayaks to experience South Moresby and neighbouring islands.

We rode our Polaris like a gently bucking horse to the first stop, north of the park reserve on Louise Island, third largest in the Charlottes. Ian Gould wanted us to see the remnants of Second World War logging of Sitka spruce to build Mosquito aircraft. Once, 200 men worked here in the thickness of the woods. Today moss and ferns cloak the rotting carcasses of Leyland trucks that ran on two-track log roads where alders now grow. Rusted gears and flanges rested in a boneyard of old machine parts. Farther along, at Mathers Creek, the helter-skelter stones of a graveyard from a century before were all that was left of a Methodist mission called New Kloo. Here some old and ailing Haida came to accept Christianity before they died of smallpox. A small column announced the grave of a Captain Skedans, who died in 1869, aged 60 years; another marker noted J. Ninstence, dead in 1896 at the age of 30. Both bore names of forsaken Haida villages that we were scheduled to see.

We crossed Cumshewa Inlet to another 19th-century village outside the park reserve on northern Moresby Island. Landing on a rocky shore and tiptoeing across bleached logs, we were amid what little remained of the winter village of Cumshewa. There were only hints of a community that, at its peak, had 450 people in at least 14 longhouses. Still, we felt a sense of peace. We stood in moss and long grass, once the interior of a house where the village began. Two corner posts had become bases for soaring conifers. Mortuary poles, their tops hollowed to hold bodies, lay at rest; one leaned in the arms of an expansive spruce. Another had fluting on the side that some believe was copied from the columns on the Parliament Buildings in Ottawa. "In 30, 40 years, there'll be very little here," Gould said.

We returned to Louise Island and Skedans, the first of the old villages where we saw a Watchman. Parks Canada was funding a program to keep Haida caretakers on important heritage sites in the South Moresby area. In the past, outsiders had to request permission to visit the sites; now, to keep tabs on the traffic passing through, people were being urged to register with Parks Canada or Haida Gwaii Watchmen offices before visiting the sites. Greeting us on shore was a 15-year-old girl in a sleeveless T-shirt and laceless sneakers, long raven hair brushing her shoulders. For five summers, Mandy Wesley had taken visitors around the site where she spent the season with

her grandparents, Charles and Caroline Wesley. They were living without running water and electricity in a wooden cabin on a big-wave beach framed by rocky outcrops. A hammock and twin clotheslines stretched between trees; a fish smokehouse suggested the food they eat. "It's never boring around here," Mandy Wesley told us in a soft yet self-assured voice. "I walk around, feed the bullheads. There's a huge bed of California mussels and I pick them and put them in the tidal pool. . . . The summer's too short."

There is a Geological Survey photograph from 1878, which is about a decade before the villagers left here for good, that shows 56 totems and 27 houses. Nearly 30 years later, far fewer of them remained when Victoria artist and writer Emily Carr recorded Skedans in words and pictures, noting that "no matter how drunken their tilt, the Haida poles never lost their dignity." They still haven't, as Mandy demonstrated in her tour of the remnants; enough survive to kindle the imagination. "You can still see the whale's tail. . . . There were four houses that were split-level, dug out at the bottom. . . . Mortuary poles were left where they fell. If too many fell, they'd actually move the village and wait for everything to deteriorate and then move back." As we strolled, the wind whipped through the tall grass, and woodsmoke from the cabin drifted over Skedans. The scent conjured up a sudden vision of what life might have been like a century and a half ago in a vital community of nearly 500 inhabitants.

Mandy's grandfather, Charles Wesley, was in his mid-seventies when we visited him. Retired from fishing and logging, he was wary when his band council asked him if he'd like to become a Watchman at Skedans. "I used to anchor here with the seiner and never went ashore," he recalled, leaning on a log on the beach. "We had weird feelings about so many of these sites where so many of our people had died in the big epidemic. We believe in some of these things, like spooks. That far end was a mass of bones and skeletons scattered all over. I'd feel all tingly. But some young people came and buried the bones. Ever since, I haven't had any weird feelings. . . . It's not a job. It's a position."

Leaving Skedans, our Polaris ran for nearly an hour into the park reserve, past evergreen island after island, mountain melting into mountain. Finally we reached de la Beche Inlet, between Darwin and Juan Perez sounds, squeezing through a dramatic cut between islands. And there it was: the dark-stained oasis of a float camp where Ian's ebullient wife, Rosie – an escapee from New York State – was waiting with iced tea and a salmon dinner. The bay is enclosed by a couple of treed islets. From the Moresby shore, there was the gentle tumbling of a stream, the only sound to be heard except for the whistles of seabirds patrolling the lightly corrugated surface of the water.

A millionaire's view from one of nature's hot tubs on Hotspring Island.

That night we roared across a glassy-calm sea for 20 minutes to Hotspring Island, which is just as exquisite as it sounds. We docked in front of the Watchmen's houses on seaweed-slick rocks, which we had to navigate in order to sign in with a Haida couple and their teenage daughter, Rosie. She took our party on a circuit of the springs, one of them a kind of enclosed metal hot tub, the others set gloriously outdoors in natural stone formations. Under a rising moon, we climbed up and over a hill through salal and blackberry bushes, bypassing the steamiest spring and a two-person pool designed for more private bathing. The medium-hot spring we did settle into could have been stolen from a scene in *South Pacific:* its millionaire's view overlooked the sea below and the mountains and islands beyond, where the sun was setting in pinks and pewters.

We didn't even mind that one of us woke up with the flu the next morning and we missed the day-long voyage through stomach-turning waves to the tiny island of Skungwai (see page 95). There, at the southernmost tip of the park reserve, perches the remote village of Ninstints, an extraordinarily preserved fragment of history. Those who went on the trip reported that more than two dozen totem poles still stand facing the sea with a magical solemnity that reminded them of the stone monoliths of another speck in the Pacific, Easter Island.

We stayed behind and sat on the dock of the float camp, with the sun bright and high, a breeze brushing the skin like a velvet glove. On the pale green mountains opposite, a slide had denuded a hillside slice of trees – nature's clearcut, and the only logging that would now be allowed in the park reserve. We felt grateful that the land of Gwaii Haanas had been saved. And missing Ninstints on this trip, we decided, would simply give us a good reason to return. One day we would come back to some of the most wild and wondrous of British Columbia's beloved islands, where – for the moment, anyway – the human and natural worlds coexist.

Windy Bay, east coast of Lyell Island, Queen Charlottes.

BOB HERGER

JANET DWYER

GUESTS AND GUARDIANS

T HE VIEW FROM THE DECK of our new home on Bowen Island is big. High on a cliff over Queen Charlotte Channel, we see south to the peninsula of Point Grey on the west side of Vancouver; east across the sea to the cliffside homes of Horseshoe Bay, where inconceivably white ferries meet as they ply three routes from Bowen and Vancouver islands; and north to the humbling beauty of mountain-rimmed Howe Sound. On spring evenings, frogs *quirk* away in our ditches. Eagles build nests in the century-old conifers below us; needle-billed flickers and jabbering jays frequent our bird feeder. As we walk up our steep driveway, black-tailed deer dart into the cedar-and-fir forest.

Everywhere we are immersed in nature. The people of our island, like those of the islands up and down this coast, feel its presence, and act accordingly. Bowen has an efficient recycling centre run by volunteers. Residents built the fish ladder that brings salmon from the sea to an inland hatchery. Islanders meet regularly as a nature club that takes them into the surrounding woods and onto the water. The two local publications carry natural history columns and stories about the active campaign to ban bow hunting of deer.

There is a sense on these islands that we are all in this together – and the *this* is a delicate environment that can be shattered by pressures of population, carelessness, and sheer stupidity. Developers have made their indelible mark on some islands, notably Saltspring; miners and loggers have scarred the skin of others, such as Texada. Yet as more people move onto these specks in the North Pacific, the ethic of conservation and caretaking – guardianship – keeps growing. The most enlightened residents, after the novelty of living amid the lushness begins to ebb, soon realize that their very existence on the islands imperils the abundance and the balance. They come to understand that we are all guests here and must try to do as little damage as we possibly can.

We must, if we are to preserve these incomparable fragments of paradise for the world.

Dionisio Provincial Park, Coon Bay, Galiano Island.

KEN STRAITON